DRAWER 345

By the Girls
Susan Crawford
Deborah Marshall

Copyright © Neleh LLC

All rights reserved. Content of this book may not be reproduced, distributed, or transmitted in any form or by any means, including photocopying, recording, or other electronic or mechanic methods, without the prior written permission of the publisher, except in the case of brief quotations embodied in critical reviews and certain other noncommercial uses permitted by copyright law. For permission requests, write to the publisher at the address below.

This book is a work of historical fiction. Any names, businesses, characters, places, or events mentioned are either products of the authors' imaginations or used in a purely fictional manner. Any resemblance to actual people, living or deceased, events, or locations is purely coincidental.

ISBN: 979-8-9923208-0-0

Authors: Susan Crawford and Deborah Marshall
Jacket design: Emilee Wiesehan
Many thanks to Danita Allen Wood and Sandy Selby for getting us across the finish line.

Printed by Lightning Press Inc. in the United States of America

First printed edition 2025

Published by:
Neleh LLC
secretsofdrawer345@gmail.com

*To Helene, Stan, Saundra, Dick,
our family, and all the people who believed in us.*

Angel number 3-4-5, communication from the divine.

3 - is the number of true potential and harmony

4 - is a sweet sign from our guardian angels to remind us we are safe

5 - means big changes and perhaps a period of self-discovery and renewed personal freedom is coming your way*

*"When the pattern for Revival is right, the glory falls,"
Dick Reuben*

*Tiny Rituals

CONTENTS

1: Stan 5

2: The Beginning 7

3: Jack and Lena Get Married 15

4: Secrets 21

5: Alma 23

6: Blanche 31

7: Orphanage 39

8: Lyle Mac 43

9: Mafia 47

10: Lyle & Lennard 51

11: Lars 57

12: Elsie 61

13: Just Love 67

14: Adoption of Stan 75

15: Orphanage to the Farm 81

16: Terry 83

17: New Beginning 91
18: Fresh Start 97
19: G.M.C. 105
20: Reube Rides 113
21: The Envelope 117
22: Stove Top 121
23: Reube's Salvation 127
24: Broken Dreams 133
25: Visit to the Farm 137
26: The Children 141
27: On Their Own 149
28: The End 155

Epilogue: Sundays With My Sissie 163
About the Authors 173
Drawer 345: Book Club 174
Book Club Questions 175

DRAWER 345

ONE
STAN

"Shorty, Shorty, oh hell, Shorty. No!"

In a second, the Triumph TR-6, number 87, race car was airborne, flying off the snake hairpin turn on the Oklahoma track. The car careened at a high rate of speed toward a hundred-year-old oak tree at the side of the racetrack. Stan's last view of life before losing consciousness was that oak tree. The sound of Stan's car crashing into the tree was deafening and could be heard around the track. Stan's mechanic, Shorty, heard the screams from the crowd and ran to the sound of the crash.

The race marshal was sitting on top of a cement building near the oak tree and saw the crash when it happened. He grabbed his walkie-talkie and screamed to Joe at the command center, "Send all help and emergency vehicles to turn number two near the big cement block by the oak tree!"

The ambulance and fire truck sped to where the car hit the tree. The crowd in the stands went silent, and the people walking across the nearby pedestrian bridge stopped and looked on in horror. When the EMTs arrived, they couldn't believe what they saw. Stan was leaning forward with his head smashed between a large tree branch and the car's roll bar. There was nothing left of the right side of his head, and the impact shattered his helmet. But Stan was still breathing.

The EMTs worked quickly to get Stan out of the car and onto the stretcher as the helicopter landed on the racetrack about 200 feet away. Shorty stood watching in stunned disbelief as his best friend was loaded into the air ambulance to head to the hospital. The EMTs were going to try everything they knew how to keep Stan alive.

TWO
THE BEGINNING

Stan's long path to that head-on crash into the oak tree started long ago, with Lena and Jack.

Lena Lake, a ravishing young beauty, was born into a lineage of wealth and societal standing. While enjoying balls and parties, she always longed for adventure. She was descended from German immigrants, and her adventurous great-great-grandfather had taken a boat down the Piney River west to settle a new town: Sells, Missouri. Her older brother, Edward, and his wife, Mae, had married and moved to Lewis, Missouri, to begin cattle farming in 1867, following the Civil War.

Lena's family owned a circus, the Lake Brothers Circus. She had three sisters—Marietta, Agnes, and Mabel—and four brothers, Karl, Edward, Stefan, and Benjamin, who died in prison in the Civil War.

Karl and Stefan Lake were entrepreneurs and put together a small traveling circus in 1871. Karl, who was Lena's favorite brother, was the frontman for the circus. He was the more polished and well-spoken brother and could communicate with the mayors and business owners, all while selling more and more tickets. Under Karl's leadership, the circus became the largest in the country. People flocked from all over the Midwest to see the acts as they traveled through Illinois, Wisconsin, Iowa, Missouri, Ohio, and other states. The circus included animals, death-defying acts, and tents full of items to purchase. Enormous crowds came out to buy tickets and merchandise.

The brothers were smart entrepreneurs, hiring former slaves and Indians as workers. These laborers worked cheaply, and they worked hard. The circus was integrated with people from all walks of life, and during the winter, their children attended school together. As the circus gained popularity around the country, exotic animals such as elephants were imported. The circus invited the public to come and see twenty-five tons of elephants along with a female bareback rider.

The circus's mode of transportation was upgraded from wagons to railroad cars in the late 1800s. When the circus train pulled into stations, it was so long that spectators couldn't see the caboose from the engine. All they could see were carnies hopping off rail cars and animals sticking their heads through the windows. The giraffe car was quite the sight with the roof cut open to accommodate the animals' long necks. The elephant cars swayed back and forth as the elephants paced, impatient to get out. With the rail cars, the circus could transport people, animals, supplies, and goods from coast to coast and throughout Europe and Australia with ease. As their fame increased and more people attended the circus, Karl and Stefan invested much of their earnings buying farmland and businesses near Topeka, Kansas. These carnies were also wealthy land barons.

As Edward and Mae began to build their farm business and new life together in Missouri, Lena was out east being entertained by many suitors who, frankly, bored her. Lena was always looking for a mate who could challenge and stimulate her mind, make her laugh, and give her love and romantic passion.

Edward always made her laugh, and she missed that. Lena had not seen her brother in years, since his wedding, so in August of 1868 she packed her clothes and took the train to visit him and his bride.

The train ride west was warm and musty, but that did not dissuade Lena from the trip. She wore a beautiful travel dress made of British brown khaki linen, resembling an outfit you would wear on safari. Her hands were covered with white gloves, and she was shaded by a parasol and a wide-brim white hat found only in the most fashionable hat stores out east. As the train arrived in Lewis, she thought to herself that this was going to be an adventure of a lifetime.

When she stepped off the train onto the platform, Lena was greeted by her brother. Edward gathered her trunks filled with clothes, linens, and perfumes, and the two walked around to the front of the train depot, where the horses and buckboard were tethered. Lena sat on the buckboard with her parasol open above her head. The ride to the farm traversed five miles of dirt road. As hard as Lena tried and as much as she fanned herself, there was no way to keep the dirt and dust off her beautiful face.

Three hours later, they arrived at the farm hungry, thirsty, and filthy. Even her curls were filled with dust and dirt from the road. Edward helped Lena off the wagon and encouraged her to go into the farmhouse to freshen up.

Edward unloaded Lena's many bags and trunks and thought to himself, *Goodness, I wonder how long she is planning to stay?*

Lena found her way to her bedroom and saw a Victorian washstand with a porcelain bowl and jug on top. Unlike in her room back home, there was no wash tub in this room. She thought she would need more than the wash bowl to clean up. But her only option was to take a sponge bath. An hour later, she finally felt presentable. She wore one of her favorite outfits, a yellow dress adorned with fabric daisies, in celebration of her visit with her brother.

Lena came downstairs and walked outside to sit on the porch and enjoy some lemonade. The family farmhand, Jack, was walking by the house when Lena walked out. He saw her and stopped dead in his tracks. *Woo Wee! She is beautiful*, he thought.

He had not seen such a fine woman in his life. He could not take his eyes off her beauty. Jack kept walking and looking over his shoulder at her. He finally made his way back to the barn to turn the horses in for the night.

That evening, Lena was sitting on the porch, drinking lemonade and admiring the beautiful Missouri sunset. As Jack approached Lena to introduce himself, he took off his hat, tipped it to Lena, and said, "Howdy, ma'am. My name is Jack Clarke. It sure is a warm day today. Mind if I join you for a glass of that lemonade?" Lena agreed, and Jack came up on the porch and sat down in the chair next to hers.

Lena wasn't sure what to think about this man, but she found him handsome. She also felt like she could trust him because he worked for the family. As she was staring off the other way from Jack, he was desperately thinking about how to make conversation.

"So, Miss Lake, how was the ride in from the train?" he finally asked.

Lena's smart-alecky reply was, "Bless your heart! You don't know how that ride was. It was dirty, bumpy, and dusty!"

Jack looked down at his hands and realized what a ridiculous question that was. She must think I am a complete idiot. Jack got up out of his chair, feeling somewhat dejected, and said, "Have a good night, Miss." He hurried down the porch and walked to the bunkhouse to turn in for the night.

The next morning, as the sun came up, Lena heard the breakfast bell ringing. She thought, *What the hell is going on? I never get up for another three hours.*

Edward banged on her bedroom door and said, "You better get up. Mae is already scrambling the eggs. The kitchen closes in thirty minutes. If you don't eat now, it will be a long time until dinner."

Lena threw back the covers and jumped out of bed. She threw on an old, ratty house coat and pants. She didn't even look in the mirror to see if she was presentable. As she ran down the stairs, fearful of missing her meal, she saw Jack at the table. She literally slid to a stop and couldn't believe he was in the kitchen.

As she gathered herself, Jack said to her, "Good morning, Miss. You are just in time for eggs and bacon."

Lena turned her back on Jack and hurried to the counter and thanked Mae for making the breakfast. After she got her food, she hesitated a bit as she walked toward the dining table and ended up sitting at the opposite end of the table from Jack. She thought to herself, *My day is not starting out well.*

As Lena was finishing breakfast, she thought, *I am so lucky that my sister-in-law opened her home to me. Mae has always been one of the kindest people in our family. Her grandparents instilled in her the values that I agree with. She is so fortunate that her grandparents encouraged her and Edward to settle and take advantage of the land grab in Henry County, Missouri, after the Civil War. Mae is a hard worker, and I know she loves my brother.*

As Lena took her dishes over to the sink after eating, Mae said to Lena, "Everyone who lives here must have a chore to keep the farm running. Your chore is cleaning up the dishes and weeding the vegetable gardens."

"Are you serious?" Lena asked.

Mae said, "Yes, I am serious! Go change your clothes. And there are big hats over in the mudroom for you to wear while you're weeding. I will need potatoes and carrots to cook for dinner."

An unhappy Lena trudged upstairs to change clothes and tie her hair back. She made her way to the vegetable garden and couldn't believe she had to dig up food. Lena decided, *Well, when in Rome, I guess I must be a farmer.*

She bent down and filled her basket with carrots and potatoes and threw weeds into a bucket to be burned. Lena's back hurt, and she sat down on the ground to take a break. Right then, a fat black snake slithered across her feet. Lena let out a blood-curdling scream that could be heard in the next county. She jumped up, and the oversized hat fell over her face. She couldn't see where she was going, and immediately ran right into Jack, who heard her screams and ran to help.

He picked her up and carried her away from the garden to get her away from the snake. As he put her down, she jerked away from him and said, "I can take care of myself."

"Well, little lady, I am not sure that is true," Jack said. He left her standing by herself and laughed on his way back to the barn. Jack couldn't help it. He fell in love with her the first night he saw her. Now he had to figure out how to win her over.

Chivalry was Jack's game plan. "After the snake incident," he said to her, "Let me show you around the farm so you know where the dangers are. I will teach you how to use a hoe and a gun to protect yourself."

Lena thought it was a good idea, but planned to act aloof. She said, "That would be fine, and I will see you tomorrow after breakfast." That night, Lena dreamed about Jack and his strong, fine body.

After breakfast, Jack and Lena rode a buckboard to the other side of the farm by the big pond. Jack had prepared a dinner bag full of sandwiches and fruit for the two of them, so they didn't have to go back to the house to eat. He showed her how to look for snakes and frogs in the water. He taught her how to hold a gun and shoot. As he put his arms around her waist to help with pointing the weapon to a target, Lena could feel her heart pounding and butterflies in her stomach.

Chivalry was working! Jack courted her with long romantic walks by the pond. They stopped to take picnics on a patchwork quilt. Jack asked Lena all about her dreams and what she wanted out of life. They read books by Charles Dickens to each other. They talked about what had happened to their country because of the Civil War. Jack challenged her intellectually, which fulfilled Lena emotionally.

One day, while taking a walk, Jack whispered to her about his life plans and his love for her. Lena had already fallen in love with Jack and wanted to spend the rest of her life with him. After eight months of courtship, Lena accepted Jack's proposal of marriage, with the blessing of Edward.

THREE
JACK AND LENA GET MARRIED

The following year, in the spring of 1869, Lena and Jack had a country wedding.

Lena's brothers and sisters traveled by train to Lewis to attend the ceremony. The women wore their finest hoop skirts and carried fans and parasols. The wedding took place on the front lawn of the farmhouse. Tables were draped with the finest linens and decorated with the family china and beautiful hydrangeas from the garden. A four-piece string quartet provided music from an impromptu stage on the wrap-around porch.

Lena's parents died in a buckboard accident before the Civil War. On that tragic day, their horses were spooked by an approaching thunderstorm and ran off the edge of the bluff into the Dublin River.

Karl was the oldest male in the family, so he walked Lena down the path, through a beautifully draped flower arch, toward Jack and the minister. As he approached the groom, Karl looked at Lena and said, "All I want is for you to be happy."

"I am," she replied.

16 | JACK AND LENA GET MARRIED

At that moment, Karl placed Lena's hand in Jack's. The ceremony was beautiful and quick. Jack and Lena kissed and walked back down the aisle after the minister pronounced them Mr. and Mrs. Clarke. They proceeded to the head table, and the guests joined them. Mae, with the help of neighbors, had prepared a bountiful buffet of finely cooked meats, casseroles, desserts, and a wedding cake adorned with white buttercream frosting and roses. The celebration lasted into the night. There was much frivolity and dancing. At 1:00 a.m., Jack and Lena said goodnight to everyone and began their new life.

A week after the wedding, all the guests were gone, and the farm was quiet. The newlyweds moved to Nebraska to chase the land rush. Jack had read about the opportunity available through the new Homestead Corn and Wheat Act, where he could claim acres of land for his own. By claiming the land, he agreed to farm it and produce crops and livestock. When Jack and Lena arrived in eastern Nebraska, they were deeded 160 acres of wide-open land near an area inhabited by Native Americans.

Fortunately, there was a town close by, so they were not completely isolated. Jack befriended local Ponca tribe members, and they taught him about the land. Their friendship grew, and Jack hired a few of them as farmhands. Lena found life on the farm difficult, but she and Jack loved the feeling of ownership and were in love and happy to be building their life together. After their first winter in Nebraska, Lena discovered she was pregnant. She was overwhelmed with joy, and so was Jack. Later that year, Lena gave birth to a son Leroy.

Jack and Lena were wonderful partners in business. They learned much from Karl about growing their landholdings and wealth. Karl often wrote letters sharing the benefits of owning land and the secrets to running a business. Jack leaned on Lena for making deals with other businessmen. She was a talented negotiator and made shrewd deals. And Lena could always smell a shyster. She was at Jack's right arm for more than thirty years and always present behind the scenes, making their business grow. Lena was also very independent, and Jack loved that about her. They began their life together on the farm with all that would fit in their wagon. In a few short years, they were prospering.

One cold, fall evening, she was in the kitchen with Leroy, now a grown, single man still living at home. They were waiting for Jack to come in from his chores for dinner. The earthy, sweet smell of leaves rustling in the wind drifted through the front door. Dusk descended, and the winds turned to the north. Lena was worried because Jack was so late. Leroy told his mother to wait in the kitchen, then took a lantern to look for his dad.

Toward the back of the farm, Leroy found his dad slumped over the edge of the wagon, his two horses standing patiently near him. Leroy realized his father was dead and fell to his knees, sobbing. He wished he could have made his dad proud, but it was too late to show him.

Leroy wondered what would become of him. He stood, picked up Jack's lifeless body, and carefully laid him in the back of the wagon. Leroy hitched the horses to the wagon and drove his father's body back to the house.

Upon arriving at the house, Leroy dropped the reins and jumped off. He ran straight into the kitchen, tears streaming down his face. "Mom, come quick. Come quick!" he screamed. "There was an accident of some sort and Dad is dead."

Lena threw open the door, ran down the steps and saw Jack in the back of the wagon. The cold wind and whipping leaves encircled her as she ran toward her husband's body. She collapsed on top of him and cried out, "No!" She shook Jack, trying to wake him, but he didn't respond.

Leroy put his hand on his mother's shoulder and told her, "Dad is gone." After a while, they moved Jack's body into the living room and Leroy drove the wagon to town to get the doctor. He knew the doctor couldn't help his father, but he thought his mother might need the doctor's help because she was crying inconsolably. When they returned, Lena was still sitting next to Jack, stroking his hair and talking to him. The doctor could see she was extremely upset, and after convincing her to rest, she went to lie down. He gave her a tonic to help her sleep.

Lena's sadness was overwhelming. She wondered what she would do now that she was a widow at age 64.

Jack's wake took place on the farm, and it was well attended. The townspeople, the Ponca tribe, and their church family attended the funeral at the local cemetery on the hill. Although the townspeople were there to support Lena and Leroy, they provided little comfort. With Jack gone, and needing money to live, mother and son sold the farm and moved to town. Leroy has never been married and had no other choice but to live with his mom. Lena was tired of caring for him and longed for her family, the balls, and the parties she remembered from her youth. She wished for the days when the family's circus wintered across the street from their home. Oh, the fun and mischief that went on.

Lena's brother Karl was such a smooth talker, and the circus was so popular that in 1902, he booked the circus to perform in the largest venue in the United States: Madison Square Garden. The shows were sold out, and the money flowed in daily. There were no financial worries for the two brothers.

With the circus performing so well, Karl felt comfortable making many visits to Kansas to check on his property. On his last visit, he fell ill while riding the train home to Ohio from Kansas. Karl was nauseous, and suffered from tingling in his hands and feet, as well as a headache. When he stepped off the train, he collapsed and died suddenly from a massive brain hemorrhage. The family sent word to Lena via telegram. After opening the message and reading about the death of her brother, Lena fainted. She could not believe her favorite brother and friend had died and left her. It was another significant loss for Lena in just two short years. She could hardly bear the pain of the loss of the one person who truly understood her. Karl knew she was a strong woman, one who could learn business, one he had hoped one day to bring into the management of The Lake Brothers Circus.

With Karl's death, the circus could not function without his leadership and business mind, and the animals were in peril if swift action was not taken. A rival circus from the East Coast made an offer for the estate, the circus's name, and all the parts of it. After the estate was settled, Karl's net worth was over $800,000—an enormous sum for the early 1900s. Per Karl's wishes, his estate was split among his four surviving sisters and his daughter.

One day a letter from the trustee and the money from Karl arrived at Lena's home. She remembered the words Karl had said. "You are smart. You are a good business person. Invest in land. It is your future."

Lena knew what to do next. As a single woman, she would buy farms and houses throughout the town and the area surrounding it. She became a land baron in her own right—wealthy, smart, and strategic.

FOUR
SECRETS

Leroy was unemployed and thirty-two years old, living at home with his mother. He had always traded on his good looks, and he got what he wanted with little effort.

From the time Leroy was born, Lena knew he differed from other children. In her heart, she felt he wasn't wired right. As a child on the farm, he was mean to animals and would abuse them in sadistic ways. His cruelty to animals was an early sign that he would struggle to have healthy relationships with people, particularly women.

Jack and Lena had many discussions about Leroy's behavior, but they could not fix him. He was a bad seed and a town bully. He had a short temper and got into fistfights with people who disagreed with him. Lena thought he suffered from some sort of mental disorder.

Unfortunately for Leroy, the only medical treatment available at the time was worse than the disease. Lena could not approve of the brain therapy that doctors wanted to perform on her son, and an institution was out of the question. She decided long ago, and promised Jack, that she would figure out a way to live with Leroy's behavior and not give up on him.

Lena was amassing a small village of properties and she needed someone to help her manage the day-to-day operations. She encouraged Leroy to learn the skills of a laborer so he could help her maintain and repair the properties she owned. She hoped he would embrace these new skills and develop some self-respect, independence, and dignity. Leroy was not having any of it.

She was surprised that he was so reluctant to grow up and earn his own way. His personality was so different from Jack's, and that was always a gut punch to Lena. Every time she thought about Jack, Lena wondered if Leroy finding his father dead exacerbated his mental struggles. She often wondered if Leroy would be different if Jack were still alive. In her heart, she knew he would be the same. She and Leroy fought often about his unwillingness to work and contribute to the family, as Lena was getting older and could not manage the farm and the properties on her own.

After a morning argument with his mother about his refusal to work, Leroy was eager to escape the conflict. He ran to the barn, harnessed the horse, and hitched it to the buckboard so he could get away from the house. He whipped the horse hard so he could flee quickly.

All he could think about was getting away from his mother.

FIVE
ALMA

Alma and her parents, James and Myrtle Kelly, arrived by train to Frances, Nebraska. When they got off the train, they grabbed their bags and luggage and walked to the Johnson County Inn on the square to stay for a few weeks until James could find a permanent farm for them to own or work. When they purchased their train tickets, the price included room and board for them at the inn, which was owned by the Union Pacific railroad company.

The next day, James walked across the square to the general store to see if anyone could help him find farmland they could afford. The general stores were usually where most of the activity happened in small towns. So, James figured the store would be a good start on his journey.

As he moseyed into the store, he saw a large man yelling at the clerk behind the cash register. "What are you talking about?" the man said in a growl. "The Clarkes only buy on credit. I don't have any cash."

Hank, the store owner, said, "We have changed our policy, and you cannot buy on credit here anymore."

Leroy threw a sack of sugar that hit Hank right behind his left ear, then stormed out of the store. James could hardly believe his ears or his eyes. He had never seen anyone with such a bad temper. Hank could barely pick himself up after being hit by the sugar, and James helped Hank get back on his feet. "Are you OK?" James asked.

"No, I am not. I hate the m-fer Leroy. He is the meanest man in town. His momma owns most of the rental property and most of the land in this area, and he thinks he can do whatever he wants, whenever he wants."

As Hank's head cleared, he realized he has not met this nice man before. "Thank you for helping me," he said. "What is your name?"

James introduced himself and explained that he and his family were new to town and looking for farmland to work. "I hoped that you folks might know who I would contact or how I would go about finding someone to help me."

Hank said, "Hey, Joe!" Joe was standing by the eggs. "Are you still looking to sell or rent your farm?"

"Yes. I am," said Joe.

Hank nodded to the newcomer. "James here is looking to work some farmland."

James and Joe left the general store and went to the local restaurant to talk more about the possibility of James renting the farm. After a few hours of talking, Joe took James out to the farm for a tour before they decided on a deal. James saw the farm had a big house, large gardens, and livestock, including horses. After taking some time to inspect the property, James said to Joe, "We have a deal."

James was so excited to tell Myrtle and Alma about their new home and the life they would begin in Frances. The family left the

Johnson County Inn the next day to start their new chapter as farmers.

Alma spent the next six weeks helping her parents get the gardens planted, the farmhouse cleaned, and the fences around the farm repaired so the cows and horses would be secured on the farm. After many long weeks of hard work, Alma's dad told her to take Sammy, the horse, for a ride in the area near the farm for the afternoon. As she put her foot in the stirrup and jumped on the saddle, she was smiling and excited to be alone and free from responsibility for a few hours.

Alma enjoyed riding Sammy on a straight dirt road, and she pushed the horse to run as fast as he could. The wind was blowing her hair behind her; she had lost her bonnet a few miles back.
She has been dreaming about this day since they got off the train. Suddenly, Alma was on the ground wondering what had just happened. She looked over and saw Sammy lying down a few feet away from her in the ditch. His leg looked broken, but she was not sure.

She heard a noise coming toward her from down the road and realized that a horse and wagon were coming down the path. Alma stood and waved her arms for help.

The noise she heard was Leroy, flying down the road in a rage. The horse was kicking dirt in his face. He barely saw the young blonde woman standing by the side of the road with a lame horse. Leroy was in a bad mood, but stopped anyway. He jerked the reins tight to get the horse to stop, then jumped off the buckboard. He stared at the girl he did not recognize, and asked if he could be of help, which was out of character for Leroy.

As he walked closer to her, she looked up and saw a tall, chiseled man with sandy brown hair and a dirty face. Her heartbeat quickened at the sight of him.

"Hi, I'm Leroy Clarke," he said. "Can I help you with your horse?"

Alma Kelly introduced herself and said, "That would be great. Can you take me to my house so my dad can come take care of the horse?"

"It would be my pleasure." Leroy helped Alma onto the buckboard. He took a rope from the back of the buckboard and walked over to the horse. He put the rope through the bit of the horse's bridle and attached it to the nearest fence post so the horse wouldn't run off. During the drive to her house, Leroy learned Alma and her family were new to town. They had arrived by train a few months ago.

Leroy realized while taking Alma home in his wagon that she was young and naive. Leroy pondered the thought that he should marry someone who does not know him. Someone like Alma. He should marry someone who thinks he is something he is not, like Alma. In his mind, he set a plan in motion to woo Alma into marrying him.

Alma's dad, James, was not happy to see Leroy coming down the lane with his daughter on the buckboard. He clearly remembered what Leroy did at the general store. He did not want his daughter to be around Leroy at all.

Alma jumped off the wagon and ran toward her father to tell him about the horse. "This nice man helped me home so I could get you to go back to take care of the horse," she said. "The horse fell to the ground. I don't really know what happened to him. It all happened so quickly."

James said to Alma, "I'm so glad you are not hurt. Now why don't you go inside with your mother."

James dismissed Leroy and told him to be on his way. James did not want a confrontation with Leroy.

A few days later, Alma walked over to the library to get a book. As she crossed the square, she saw Leroy walking toward her. He recognized her instantly and said, "Howdy, Miss! It's been awhile since I saw you last. How are things on your farm?"

Alma's heart was beating so quickly, she barely heard a word he said. Her feelings for him were rushing over her. Leroy invited Alma to sit on the bench outside the library. They sat for hours talking, and Alma forgot all about the book she was going to check out. Suddenly, Alma realized how late it was and that she must get home.

Leroy was sad she had to go. He took her by the hand and asked, "Can I come by the farm to call on you?"

As she was running across the square, she yelled, "I can't wait!"

The next week, Leroy made a call to Alma's home and asked her father if he could spend some time with her on the farmhouse porch. James was not happy about the request but allowed Leroy to spend time with Alma that evening. It was a warm night, and the lemonade Alma made for him tasted so sweet. As they talked about their life dreams and their families, all Leroy could think about was marrying Alma. He thought, *I have to hurry so she does not get to know the real me.*

His courtship was nothing but a charade. He knew Alma must not see his temper before they married. All the while, James had seen the real side of Leroy. The courtship continued for about three more months, and Leroy was getting impatient. He and Alma planned a night for him to come to her bedroom window and get her. On a rainy evening about a week later, he came by her home in the middle of the night and whisked Alma away from the farm to elope.

After eloping to the nearby town, Alma and Leroy moved into one of Lena's rentals near the town square.

Alma quickly realized she made a mistake in marrying Leroy. Life is not as she thought it would be. She was frightened every day. Leroy would wake up and berate her just for breathing. He would push her to the ground and force himself upon her. She would hold her breath, hoping he would not kill her. One day, he had to go to his mother's house to help with one of the farm animals. Alma knew this was her only chance. She grabbed her shawl and ran as fast as she could to her parents' home. When her dad opened the door, he saw the bruises on her face and the thinness of her body.

Alma never saw Leroy again.

James raced straight to town to Leroy's home and confronted him about the abuse of his daughter. Leroy knocked James to the ground outside of the house. The two got into a fistfight and then Leroy pulled a gun on Alma's father and fired, just missing James's head. James ran and found the sheriff. The sheriff and James went back to Leroy's house, and the sheriff arrested Leroy for firing a weapon at an unarmed man in the city limits, and for marrying Alma without her father's permission.

The residents of the town did not like Leroy. They knew he was a bully. They disapproved of Leroy marrying Alma. The townspeople were right. Word spread quickly that Leroy had abused Alma, and their marriage was annulled by the local pastor at the Lutheran

Church. Alma's family had been seen at the train station with all their suitcases, running away for a fresh start for her.

Leroy walked around town like he was oblivious to the townspeople's stares and disgust. His mother was also disappointed in him as she never imagined that she would have raised a son like him. Leroy could not find meaningful work or hold a job, abused women, and lived rent-free in one of Lena's homes. Lena realized she had enabled him to be the person he had become. She knew that if Jack were still there, maybe together they could have turned Leroy around.

SIX

BLANCHE

Leroy needed farming supplies and took the train to the neighboring town of Nemaha to buy the supplies. While on the train, he pulled out the hundred dollars his mother had given him to buy supplies. He knew, deep down, that he was beholden to Lena for everything he had, which made him feel less of a man. The train stopped, and he jumped off and walked to Waters Feed Store. That was where he saw a beautiful young woman. She had dark hair and eyes and was tall, long-legged, and unlike any woman he had seen.

The woman saw Leroy, and he looked nothing like anything she had seen before either.

Leroy thought to himself again, *Here is a woman who knows nothing about me. Maybe this one will work.* He introduced himself and started up a conversation.

He had figured out that the only people who would have anything to do with him were those who didn't know he was a fake and a fraud. He was sure he could fool this young woman too.

He learned her name: Blanche. She told him that her family lived in town, behind the cemetery. Leroy was attracted to Blanche and wanted to spend some time with her. He asked if he could stop by her parents' home to visit with her.

She said yes, hopeful that her parents, Dee Dee and Harry, would allow it.

Leroy had a change of plans. The supplies would have to wait until tomorrow. Leroy rented a room at the local boarding house.

Leroy arrived at Blanche's house around nightfall. He had bathed, and his good looks showed. Blanche's father, Harry, answered the door and did not appear pleased that this older man was asking for his daughter. To him, Leroy looked middle-aged. Against his better judgment, Harry let Leroy in.

Over the next six months, Blanche fell madly in love with Leroy—much to her parents' chagrin.

Leroy tried not to make the same mistake he had made with Alma. Blanche was unaware of his previous marriage, as it had been annulled. He picked Blanche up after church one Sunday and they took the train to Frances so he could introduce her to his mother. They went to Lena's house and sat on the porch to visit. Lena immediately favored Blanche for her intellect, quick wit, and strong backbone. She thought to herself, *Blanche is just like me*. Lena asked Leroy to come by her house after he took Blanche home. She was feeling like her days ahead were shorter, and she wanted to leave some legacy of her life behind. She gave Leroy her wedding ring from Jack and gave her blessing for him to ask Blanche to marry him.

Feeling emboldened by his mother's confidence in him, he asked Harry for Blanche's hand in marriage.

Harry and Dee Dee told Leroy they did not approve of his relationship with Blanche or of the marriage. Blanche was Jewish and Leroy was a Christian, and those two religions could not easily intertwine in the early 1900s. Blanche's parents had also heard town gossip about the bully from the neighboring town, and they realized those rumors were about Leroy. They knew the marriage would be doomed from the beginning.

Leroy and Blanche ran away and eloped, just like he had done before. This infuriated her parents, and they disowned Blanche. By marrying a man of another faith, she was as good as dead to them. Lena was not happy that Jack and Blanche had eloped, or that Blanche's parents disapproved. But Lena let them live in the small, one-bedroom house she owned by the town square, but she knew people in town would shun the couple. Blanche was the only Jewish person in the town. Neither of them would have a place to worship.

The marriage was rocky, not only because of religious differences, but because Leroy had returned to being the bully everyone knew him to be. He would not let Blanche leave the house and would push her down and hit her, just as he had with Alma. Blanche got pregnant right away after they were married, and gave birth to her first daughter, Elizabeth.

Leroy refused to let Lena visit their home, as he did not want his mother to see the havoc he had created in his marriage. He knew if she saw Blanche in the deplorable condition she was in and the filth in their home, Lena would take Blanche to her home for refuge. And because Lena never came to visit, she had no relationship with her granddaughter. Blanche could have used Lena's help and love, especially since her parents had written her off and Leroy had no job or money of his own.

A few months after Elizabeth was born, Blanche was pregnant again. Shortly after the birth of the couple's second daughter, Anne, Leroy went to see Lena. He needed help and money. There was little to eat in their home, the kids were cold, and neither girl had shoes.

As he drove to Lena's country farm, he realized he had not seen his mother for a long time. He looked around the home and everything was out of place. It looked dark and uninviting. The door was unlocked, and he opened it to walk in. He hollered, "Mom, Mom, Mom!"

The smell was overwhelming. He saw Lena in the chair. She had obviously been dead for a long time.

Lena's funeral took place the following week. No one came from town. There was no support for Leroy or his family. The minister was brief and aware there was a Jewish woman in the pew. After the funeral, the wagon carrying Lena's body headed up the hill to the cemetery so she could be laid to rest near her beloved Jack.

Leroy inherited his mother's wealth, but it was tied up in land. With the impending war, Leroy could not sell the land for cash to take care of his family. The local bank would not lend him money with the land as collateral.

When Leroy was cleaning out his mother's home, he found that Lena had stashed away about $725 throughout the house—under her bed, and in coffee cans in the kitchen.

Filled with grief over the next few weeks, Leroy's tirades increased. Having found both his parents dead had contributed to his out-of-control mental illness. He forced himself on the now emaciated Blanche, and she became pregnant for the third time. She delivered a baby boy, James, nine months later. Leroy was never happy. He did not take care of the children and he only thought of himself.

Leroy had been unemployed for so long and was drinking away the cash Lena had stashed away in her home before she died. Blanche found anything she could kill to eat so the children would not starve to death. She was not above begging from neighbors for help. Unfortunately, very few neighbors could help because they had so little themselves.

A year after James was born, in 1918, the Spanish flu reached pandemic levels across the Midwest. Everyone in the family was stricken with the flu. The local doctor did a welfare check on Leroy and his family and was appalled by what he saw. He reported his findings to the local newspaper, describing the poor living conditions and squalor that Leroy's family were living in.

The report in the newspaper sent Leroy into a rage. Sick with flu and fever, he stormed into the doctor's office and screamed, "How dare you report on my family, embarrassing me in front of the entire town? You could have provided us with some help, medicine, or food, not just judged."

The doctor replied, "You embarrassed yourself and are unfit to be a husband and parent." A few weeks later, Blanche died from the Spanish flu, leaving the three children alone with Leroy.

After Blanche's funeral, the elders of the town deemed Leroy unfit to be a parent. They gave him one option: to send the children to an orphanage in Iowa. The doctor encouraged this action. He knew the children would not be safe under Leroy's care. Leroy never loved his children, and the decision to give them up was easy for him—a relief, really. He sent the girls to the orphanage in Iowa, but not the baby boy. Leroy was a greedy man and sold the little boy, James, to a family in the next town.

Elizabeth and Anne, seven and five years old, were put on the train by themselves. They were two little girls who had just lost their mom and brother. All they had with them was a small bag of clothes and some food for the train ride. Leroy did not even hug them goodbye; he just stood on the platform as the two walked up the steps into the train car. Elizabeth sat by the window and Anne sat next to her. Tears rolled down their faces. They could see their dad standing there as the train departed the station. He turned his back and walked away, having never even waved goodbye.

As the train pulled away, Anne and Elizebeth held each other tight. They did not know what was ahead. Who would take care of them? Where would they sleep? Would these people be nice? How would they know if the people meeting them at the next stop were decent? So many questions.

The train the girls were put on was often known as an 'orphan train' and it would take six hours for them to get to their new home. Orphan trains were designed to move children from their parents to orphanages or foster care. Between 1854 and 1929, more than 200,000 American children were put on orphan trains in the country. The train ride was not fun and Elizabeth and Anne were cold and scared. There were scary men on the train who stopped by their seats and bullied them. Anne screamed as a strange man pulled her out of her seat and dragged her down the aisle. Elizabeth ran to the conductor to get help, and the conductor grabbed the man and stopped the train. The man was thrown off the train and met by authorities for arrest. Anne and Elizabeth held on to each other and knew they would never leave each other's side. Elizabeth also knew that she was now the oldest of the family and had to protect her younger sister.

The train finally stopped, and Elizabeth and Anne were in a small town in Iowa. There were rolling hills and large trees. They could smell the farms and see pigs and cows and crops for miles. Out the window of the train, they saw two women wearing long dresses with aprons and bonnets standing on the platform. They watched as one of the women came into the rail car, walked right to them, and asked, "Are you Elizabeth and Anne?" From that moment on, their lives were changed. They would never see or talk to their father again. These women were their parents now, and Iowa was their new home.

The children were gone, and the season had changed. Leroy learned from a banker in Kansas that he was an extremely wealthy man. Lena had been the businesswoman her brother Karl knew she could be. She employed a financial institution in Kansas because she didn't trust the local banks in Frances to protect her money. Her financial adviser, Scott, in Kansas, was a savvy broker who helped her make substantial investments that brought her the return she was looking for.

All by herself, with Scott's guidance, she had amassed a fortune in money and property worth over $300,000, a doubling of the money Karl had left her. She had left it all to Leroy, who did not really know what to do with it. Scott, Lena's financial investor, knew that Leroy could not handle the money that was in his mother's estate. Lena had made Scott the adviser and distributor with instructions to care for Lena's grandchildren as well.

Leroy did not tell anyone about his inheritance, and he packed up his few belongings and moved away. The last thing he did was send the Sears and Roebuck catalog to the orphanage in Iowa, where the girls were, with a note attached: "Order whatever you need. It will be paid for." Over the years, the girls never knew where the additional catalogs came from or who paid for what they bought. Scott agreed to keep everything a secret at Lena's request.
They never got to know their grandparents, brother, or father, and they missed their mother terribly.

So many secrets. So many lies. So much destruction. The order of life undone.

SEVEN
ORPHANAGE

Elizabeth dreamed of a life without illness, death, and squalor, and she shared that dream with Anne. The memory of the two of them finding their mother lifeless, cold, disfigured, and torn down by life was emotionally haunting. As the girls cried over the death of their mother, their father offered no comfort and spent his time drinking to deaden his own pain. He told them repeatedly that he hated them and did not want to care for them. The mental abuse was so severe that, even as children, they wanted to retaliate against him.

The Swedish Lutheran home, where the girls were sent, was on a beautiful, windy 240 acres of Iowa pasture. The home was a ministry for John Smithsson and his wife, who emigrated from Sweden in the late 1800s. There were two ten-room homes that sat next to each other, one for girls and one for boys, and a grass farm filled with goats, cows, chickens, and pigs. There were about fifty children who lived there, and each had daily chores to keep the farm going. The girls did the cooking and sewing, and the boys tended to the land and animals. Besides working on the farm, the children attended daily classes in a one-room schoolhouse and went to church each Sunday at the nearby Markel Lutheran Church.

The adults who ran the home were loving and orderly. However, there was a high expectation that the children would show respect and topline manners each day.

Elizabeth and Anne realized this would be their home for many years. They were lonely and timid as they had been through so much worry and tragedy following the death of their mother. But after living in squalor and despair for so long, the welcoming decor and colors of the home made Elizabeth and Anne finally feel safe.

It was the dead of winter when they arrived, cold and hungry. The home smelled musty, like it needed to be aired out, which was impossible since there were five inches of snow on the ground.

After they got something to eat, Elsa, the superintendent, took the girls upstairs and showed them the dormered room where they would live. The space was filled with rows of white metal beds topped with thin mattresses and one blanket. If anyone had any belongings, they were stowed under the beds. The girls only had one suitcase between them. Elsa helped them pick out beds near each other. There were dust bunnies everywhere. Elizabeth thought to herself, *The first thing I am going to do tomorrow is to sweep and dust everywhere.* She cleaned the house when they lived with their father, Leroy. For a seven-year-old, Elizabeth had lived the life of an adult.

Elsa told the girls, "We are going to take care of you like no one ever has. Don't worry. You will be warm and will have food to eat. Oh, yes, I almost forgot. Someone sent a Sears and Roebuck catalog for you. You are to order whatever you need. It will be paid for." She handed them the catalog to look at. Elizabeth knew the first things she was going to order were a new pillow, blanket, and undergarments.

The first night, as they lay in bed, Elizabeth and Anne held hands and cried themselves to sleep. They were frightened and felt hopeless. The other girls picked on them during dinner. They were starving and exhausted. Dinner that night was basic vegetables and some meat, but there were no seconds. They hoped tomorrow would be a better day.

The following morning, Elizabeth awoke and was the first one downstairs. She found Elsa in the kitchen, preparing breakfast for all the girls. Elsa was tall and a little plump. She was a strong, solid Lutheran woman. As Elizabeth sat at the counter, Elsa asked her how she was doing. Elizabeth said, "I am not doing so well. I don't understand why I am here. I am hungry, cold, tired, and feel abandoned."

Elsa hugged Elizabeth and said, "Trust me, everything will be OK." They made small talk until the other girls came down. This became their morning routine. Each day, Elizabeth would get up before everyone and enjoy her time alone with Elsa.

Elsa quickly recognized that Elizabeth was intelligent and had many talents. The youngster loved handwork and made beautiful quilt pieces. One of Elizabeth's favorite squares was a dusty rose pink and green combination. Every day as they talked, Elsa worked to instill confidence in Elizabeth, to nurture her, her sewing skills, and her spirits.

The summer after the girls arrived, during one of their early morning conversations, Elizabeth confided to Elsa about the treatment they received from their father and how their mother had died. While Elsa knew some of this, she did not know the extent and the damage Elizabeth and Anne's father had caused to their mental and physical health. Elsa became very close to Elizabeth and worked daily to help her get through the loss of their mother and the trauma she and her sister had endured. As the years went on, Elizabeth learned so much from Elsa, who was a loving, wonderful maternal figure.

At age 15, the children at the home "aged-out" and become adults in the eyes of the ministry. As young people, they were then required to find employment and housing elsewhere. Elizabeth's feelings about leaving differed from the feelings she had as a seven-year-old when she arrived. Leaving the home was bittersweet. Everyone there had become her family and support system—most of all, Elsa. She would have to leave Anne behind, as she was not old enough to leave. Most of the 15-year-old girls became nannies for wealthy families, and the boys became farmhands.

The Swedish home was a gift to so many and saved many lives. In the early 1940s, it closed its doors, and the ministry was abandoned.

EIGHT
LYLE MAC

In the spring of 1917, a young man from Oak Leaf, Iowa, headed to State College to avoid the First World War. Lyle Mac was sixteen years old and had his whole life in front of him. He dreamed of becoming a revered businessman and the first step was to go to college.

Lyle was a troubled soul, though. He was plagued by memories of his parents who, angry because he spoke back to them, beat him in the horse barn with a whip. His sister Roberta often mouthed back to their parents and endured the same fate but did not survive the beatings. One night, after a beating from her dad, Roberta went into the horse barn, climbed the stairs to the top of the hayloft, threw a rope over the rafter in front of her and tied it tight. She made a noose with the rope and put it around her neck. Then she stepped forward and threw herself off the loft. She was fourteen.

Lyle found his sister hanging, covered in dust, with a black and blue face and multiple bruises. He realized he needed to get away from his parents if he hoped to escape the beatings and live. It was a memory that haunted Lyle every day.

While at State College, Lyle joined the Sigma Chi fraternity and spent most of his time playing cards, smoking cigars, and drinking whiskey. His grades reflected his lack of focus. Fortunately for

Lyle, he met Johannes Mueller in chemistry class. Johannes set the grading curve for the class and Lyle has asked if Johannes would tutor him to help him catch up. They became fast friends, and Lyle's grades improved in chemistry class.

By 1918, World War I had taken so many American casualties that even college boys like Johannes and Lyle were drafted to fight. The friends were sent to France near the Alsace region. When they arrived at their camp, they saw how poor the conditions were, even before they started fighting. The units were housed in tents with wood floors laid on top of the dirt. They could feel the cold, wet air coming up through the floor under their feet. The tents had no heat or any way to stay warm except for the issued blanket on their assigned cots. On the south wall was an easel. Hanging from a board were the dog tags of all the men who died at the front. Lyle began to sweat as he approached that heartbreaking display and read the names and ages on the tags. He and Johannes were the same age. The two of them felt anxious and terrified about what might happen to them.

They ended up on the French/German line, near Saarbrucken, which was close to where Johannes's family was from. They spent many nights in freezing cold trenches talking about their beliefs. Johannes's family immigrated to Ohio from Germany in the mid-1800s. They were escaping wars, persecution, and economic hardships. Johannes's family had been involved in the uprising of the antisemitic movement in Germany, and those beliefs were ingrained in Johannes as a young child.

One night in the trenches during a bombing raid by the Allies, over the border in Germany, Lyle and Johannes talked about their lives amid the explosions. Johannes told Lyle that he believed in an Aryan race and was positive that white, intelligent men should always be in control of money, religion, and government. He believed he would have biological children who would carry this belief into the future.

Toward the end of 1918, Germany was on the verge of chaos and upheaval. As a result, Kaiser Wilhelm II abdicated and asked the Allies for an armistice. Germany became a republic with a new leader, Chancellor Friedrich Ebert, and the war ended. The unexpected conclusion of the war led to problems with getting troops mobilized and home. Spanish Flu raged around the world, which made it difficult for the soldiers to get home. American servicemen were sent to the French countryside to wait until ships were available to bring them back from Europe.

After four months of living in the French countryside, Johannes and Lyle received their orders to board the *Mount Vernon* troop ship that would sail across the Atlantic to the United States. They arrived in early 1919, and wondered what the country was going to be like. Once they landed in New York, they discovered that prohibition was the law of the land and the Spanish Flu had ravaged the country. They did not know what they were going to find when they got back home to the Midwest. One thing was for sure: the smell of blood and burning flesh and the destruction of war was seared into their memories and would haunt them forever.

Little did Lyle and Johannes know their paths would cross, both personally and professionally, for the next thirty years.

NINE
MAFIA

In 1909, Congress passed an amendment to the Homestead Act of 1862: The Enlarged Homestead Act. The Act of 1862 provided any adult citizen or intended citizen who had never taken arms up against the government with 160 acres of land.

The Enlarged Homestead Act doubled the allotted land people could attain from the Act of 1862, increasing acreage from 160 to 320 acres.

In the early 1900s, the Mafia was in full force in Iowa. Nearly every business deal made in the state ran through one of the Iowa Mafia families—Cosenza, Amalfi, and Sarenta. Their ties to the Chicago Mafia families ran deep with money and blood. Plenty of businesses in Iowa needed the blessings of those families to succeed.

The Iowa Mafia saw this amendment as an investment opportunity for their bootleg liquor business, R.O.I. Feed and Grain. They sought and got 3,200 acres of land that would be sectioned off for various types of crops. Now, all they needed were farmers to work the land.

The Iowa Mafia placed classified ads in newspapers throughout Iowa and surrounding states looking for workers. Lynnard

Mac, who was unemployed and living in Council Bluffs, saw an advertisement in his local newspaper seeking farmers and farm hands to work near Oak Leaf, Iowa. Lynnard was excited by the possibility of employment and the opportunity to feed his family. He answered the classified ad via a telegram sent somewhere near Sioux City.

A couple of days later, he received a telegram back from R.O.I. Feed and Grain asking him to take the train to Sioux City to finalize the details of contract work for that company near Oak Leaf.

Two weeks later, Lynnard moved his family and began to farm the new 320-acre homestead. He would grow corn, barley, wheat, and rye for his new employer. Lynnard's son Lyle was tasked with cutting trees on the farm to be milled for a new farmhouse and horse barn. For the next six years, Lyle worked hard on the farm trying to please his dad, but it was never enough.

While Lyle was overseas fighting in the war, Lynnard struggled with his commitment to produce crops for R.O.I. Feed and Grain. There had been a drought for a couple of years and Lynnard lost most of his farm hands to the war.

One day, while working out in the fields to make something of this farm, Lynnard saw a car drive up the lane. He did not recognize it. Two huge, burly men got out of the car and walked toward him. They were dressed in three-piece suits and wore tweed fedoras. Their shoes were dark brown with buckles that shone in the sun. Lynnard was nervous about the situation in front of him. He didn't know who those guys were, but they knew him.

The driver of the car, Max, said to Lynnard, "You need to come with us."

Lynnard backed away from the two men, grabbed his shotgun and said, "Get off my land."

The car's passenger, Harry, pulled out a gun and said, "This is not your land, and the man who owns it wants to speak with you, now."

Lynnard turned and ran toward the house, but slipped on gravel and fell. The two men ran up next to him, grabbed him by his ankles and dragged him to the car. They opened the back door and threw him in the back seat. As they drove away, Harry pointed his gun at Lynnard and told him not to move or his head would be gone.

A few hours later, they arrived in Sioux City at R.O.I. headquarters. Max and Harry dragged Lynnard out of the car and hauled him into a deserted building. There was only one light turned on, but in it, Lynnard saw a big, fat man standing about fifty feet from him. He did not know who the man was or why he was in Sioux City.

Max said to the fat man, "Babe, here is your guy. What do you want us to do now?"

"Sit him down in that chair and go outside." Babe said with a cigar hanging out of his mouth. Smoke billowed all around him and he was sweating. He ambled slowly across the room toward Lynnard, grabbed the terrified man by his overalls, and said, "Do you know why you are here?"

"No," Lynnard said.

"Do you think you are farming the land you are on for yourself?"

Lynnard looks at Babe with terror in his eyes and, with a shaky voice, answered, "I don't really know who I farm the land for. I thought it was R.O.I. Feed and Grain."

Babe let go of Lynnard and his enormous belly shook as he laughed. "You stupid farmer, you have no idea who you work for. The land you work is owned by the Iowa Mafia, and you owe us because you have not turned a crop for two years. For every year you don't produce a crop, you owe me twice what the crop is selling for. You owe us $10,000 to date for lack of production."

"I don't have that kind of money," Lynnard said, "and I had no idea that I would owe you anything. I quit!"

"Oh no," Babe said and shook his head. "When you signed the contract, you signed an agreement for the money, and death is the only way out of it."

Babe pulled Lynnard out of the chair and threw him out the door to Max and Harry. "You have been warned," he said to Lynnard, "and you will start paying me back $100 per month until your debt is paid with interest. Max and Harry will come by the first of each month to collect."

Max and Harry threw him to the ground and gave him a few kicks in the gut for emphasis. Lynnard pulled himself up off the ground but couldn't stand. His gut hurt so badly that he threw up on Max's shiny shoes. Max retaliated with a punch to Lynnard's face and threw the dazed man in the back of the car. Max and Harry drove him to the train station, bought him a ticket, and sent him back to Oak Leaf.

TEN
LYLE & LYNNARD

It was late in 1919 when Lyle and Johannes returned to the United States. They were excited to be back in the US and quickly disembarked from the *Mount Vernon*. The friends spent the next two days in New York City, living it up and seeing all that the city offered. From there, they took the train to Chicago, and Johannes traveled on to Ohio to visit some of his family. Lyle begrudgingly went back to Oak Leaf. Returning to college was out of the question, as everyone had to work to make up for the war.

Lyle's father met him at the train station. His father wasn't sure what his son looked like anymore since he had not seen him for years. He recognized Lyle as he walked off the train and couldn't believe his son had become such a handsome, grown man. He was much taller and thinner than Lynnard remembered.

Lyle was not excited to see his father. The last time he saw him, his sister had just died. He felt his dad couldn't have cared less about him, especially when he left for the war. Now that he saw his father, he thought, *He looks old and worn out. The years have not been kind to him.*

Lyle walked toward his father and felt incredibly awkward. He didn't know what to say to him. All he wanted to do was rent a room at the local boarding house and sleep, but his dad was in the way. "Thanks for meeting me at the station," he said, "but I really want to rest for a while and get my bearings back. Could we meet for coffee in a few days to catch up?"

Lynnard was disappointed. "Sure."

A few days later, Lynnard and Lyle met at the local bakery for coffee. Lynnard invited the owner of the bakery, Izzy, Babe's cousin, to have coffee with them. He wanted to introduce Izzy to his son. Over the past eighteen months, Lynnard had been making his loan payments to Babe through Izzy. Izzy knew it had been tough for Lynnard to make the payments, and they had worked out a deal for Lyle to work for Izzy and pay off part of Lynnard's debt by holding out money from Lyle's check. Lyle would never know about the arrangement. During coffee, Izzy offered Lyle a job as a baker and store manager. Lyle accepted and started work the next day.

Lyle was unaware he would be paying off his father's debt and had no idea who he was really working for.

Lyle, surprisingly, enjoyed working at the bakery. He was making enough money to pay his own bills and began to feel like part of the community. Izzy thought Lyle had a lot more potential than being a baker and a store manager. He saw that Lyle had good business acumen and managed the books of the bakery well. Because Lyle was doing so well, Izzy sent a telegram to Babe and asked him to come to Oak Leaf to talk about Lyle's future.

Babe went to Oak Leaf to visit the bakery and see if Lyle would be a good fit for the Iowa family business. As far as Babe knew, Lyle didn't know about the Mafia connections with the bakery or his father.

While at the bakery, Babe asked Lyle to go to dinner with him at his brother's Italian restaurant in Oak Leaf. Izzy came along.

That night, they ordered garlic bread, spaghetti and meatballs, lots of wine, and tiramisu. The table was covered in a red and white checked tablecloth that had old wine bottles with dripping candles stuck in the tops. They drank wine and discussed Lyle's future in the business. Babe told Lyle that he thought he would make a fine businessman, and he wanted the young man to be part of his company.

"I am flattered," Lyle said, "but I would like to think about your offer overnight."

The next day, Lyle was at work when Babe came into the bakery for breakfast and a good cup of coffee. Izzy sat down with Babe and told him, "The local flour mill is up for sale. What would you think if we backed Lyle to purchase the mill?"

Babe thought to himself, *I will have it all. Grains and flour at my disposal. With this, I could control almost all the food production in Iowa.*

Babe said to Izzy, "You are my favorite nephew. Let's get the mill and the boy into the business."

Lyle Mac purchased the flour mill in 1921, with Mafia family money. After purchasing the flour mill, he became the most sought after bachelor in town. A French socialite, Genevieve, who had ties to Chicago crime families, caught his attention at a local dance. She had arrived in Oak Leaf shortly after Lyle went to work at the bakery. She was there for one purpose only: to capture Lyle's attention.

Lyle had no idea she was a plant sent by the crime families. She was there to make sure Lyle did what he was supposed to do. Lyle courted Genevieve and fell madly in love with her. The two got married eight months later. The wedding was a high-society affair and was the talk of Iowa. There were many out-of-town guests that arrived by train. The wedding was lavish, and no expenses were spared. Wine, bourbon, and many delicacies were imported from the French countryside.

In 1926, life was going well for Lyle and Genevieve. They were the most admired couple in Oak Leaf and invited to the society parties. Lyle was awarded the flour contract by the governor to manufacture flour for the entire state of Iowa. He became even more wealthy and powerful after getting the contract, as did the Mafia. He used his influence as vice president and board member of the Rotary Club to further his wealth and connections in Iowa.

Their family began to grow when Lyle and Genevieve had a daughter, Alexandra, in 1928. Lyle felt that his family was complete with the addition of Alexandra. However, Genevieve was bored and wanted her old society life back. She wanted to go to the country club, to Europe, shop endlessly, have tea with friends, and pamper herself. She implored the Mafia bosses to let her go, as this life in Oak Leaf was more than she bargained for with them.

Genevieve despised being a mother, and she did not have the skills, nor did she want to take care of their daughter. All the while, energetic Alexandra was showing all the signs of genius level thinking at age two. She read at a kindergarten level and was beginning to learn the French language. Genevieve's failure to bond with Alexandra and her unwillingness to care for her had put a strain on Genevieve's marriage with Lyle.

When Alexandra was two years old, Lyle went to the Swedish boarding house, which was 30 miles away, where children who were orphaned by the loss of parents to the Spanish flu or parents who could not care for their children lived. He surveyed all the girls and asked many questions about their intelligence and nurturing abilities. Lyle wanted to find a servant to care for Alexandra, since Genevieve refused to do so.

The superintendent of the orphanage assured him there was only one girl he should pick. Her name was Elizabeth Clarke, and she was sixteen years old. Elizabeth had been at the orphanage with her sister Anne since she was seven.

Lyle met her and knew right away that she was the one. He brought Elizabeth home as a servant and teacher for Alexandra, and assumed guardianship of Elizabeth until she was twenty-four. Genevieve was unhappy that Lyle brought home a girl from an orphanage to take care of their daughter. She was also a bit jealous of Elizabeth's beauty and smarts. Genevieve's mood continued to be unhappy, and she pouted because no one paid attention to her. She refused to play a part in her daughter's life.

Several years went by and Alexandra was thriving and getting ready for kindergarten. She loved Elizabeth, but Elizabeth was eager to move on with her own life.

ELEVEN
LARS

Elizabeth continued to ponder her life and wondered about her future as the country reeled from the Great Depression. It was 1932, and Prohibition still had a foothold in the United States. Unemployment was 24 percent, and people were living on the streets. Charles Lindbergh's child was kidnapped, and the ramifications of banks going out of business and drought were felt everywhere. The Chicago gangsters had control of illegal alcohol and groceries in the Midwest, most notably Al Capone's hold on Sioux City, Iowa. Alcohol and speakeasies were abundant in this gateway-to-the-West town.

In the spring, three years after becoming Alexandra's nanny, Elizabeth was excited about finishing high school. Elizabeth graduated with honors from Oak Leaf High School, where her classmates gave her the name "Swede." Also noted in the yearbook next to her picture was her favorite three letter word: M.E.N. Elizabeth was boy-crazy and a bit of a flirt. Her friends thought she was quite the character.

Elizabeth's daily nanny duties changed after high school. Alexandra went to kindergarten full time, and Elizabeth had to find a part-time job. Besides her nanny duties, she held down a part-time job as a secretary at the Mac family's Logle flour mill.

She enjoyed her work at the flour mill and learned a lot about the business from Lyle. Elizabeth felt lucky to be employed and to have a roof over her head when so many people were out of work and struggling.

Her job at the mill gave Elizabeth the opportunity to meet the people who come through the door. One day, a salesman from Sioux City, Lars Gustafsson, arrived by train to Oak Leaf to meet with Lyle and negotiate a better price on flour for his family's grocery store up north.

Lars was young, handsome, and debonair. As he walked into the mill office, he whisked his fedora off his head and the second he laid eyes on Elizabeth, said, "Well, hello, Miss."

Elizabeth returned his gaze with her big brown eyes, and said, "Hello, sir. May I help you?" She was dressed in a sexy, short-sleeved, green and black plaid dress with stockings and high heels. Elizabeth knew how to put an outfit together after all those years of looking through the Sears and Roebuck catalog with Anne. She was a beauty.

Lars explained he was there to see Lyle. Elizabeth stood and led him to the boss's office. As she walked down the hallway, Lars followed, carrying his hat under his arm, and all he could think about was her.

After meeting with Lyle, Lars got back on the train to Sioux City, but he couldn't get Elizabeth off his mind.

A couple of weeks later, he came up with an excuse to his boss that he needed to go back to Oak Leaf. His only reason for the trip was to see Elizabeth again. He arrived at the Logle Milling Company unannounced and was thrilled to see Elizabeth sitting at the reception desk. He took a deep breath and asked Elizabeth if she would have dinner with him that night. Not knowing if she would say yes or no, Lars had packed a light overnight bag with a change of clothes, toothbrush, shaving kit, and special goodies he could only get in Sioux City.

Elizabeth accepted his invitation and said she can join him after work.

Lars was waiting for her after work in the parking lot. They walked to the station and took the train to the next town to dine. During dinner, as Elizabeth and Lars talked, they began to feel like they had known each other their entire lives. They shared many of the same ideas and values and were comfortable with each other. As Elizabeth talked, Lars heard nothing as he stared into her eyes, desiring her lips, and dreaming about caressing her breasts. He thought, *This is the woman I have been waiting for my entire life. I have to have her.*

Elizabeth's legs quivered as they continued to share their hopes for the future. Lars's ocean-blue eyes pulled Elizabeth in deep. Both their hearts were racing, and romance was on their minds. After they finished dessert, Lars reached across the table to hold Elizabeth's hand and said, "Let's get out of here!"

They left the restaurant holding hands, and Lars invited Elizabeth to come back with him to his boarding house for the night. She agreed, and the secret began.

TWELVE
ELSIE

In early 1931, Lyle visited Grimes, Iowa, to see his old Army buddy, Johannes Mueller. Johannes and Lyle had been communicating through letters since they got back from the war. In those letters, Lyle shared how he had amassed a fortune upon returning from the war. After marrying Genevieve, he wrote to Johannes that he was affiliated with the Iowa Mafia and managed and owned a large flour mill in Oak Leaf. He told Johannes about his relationship with the Mafia, which had been arranged by his dad. His dad owed the Mafia a lot of money, and Lyle was paying off his father's debt. He hoped the outstanding debt would be resolved by 1935. But he was worried that the debt would never be paid off and he would always be in debt to the Iowa Mafia because of the flour mill and his father.

Through letters back from his friend, Lyle learned that Johannes and his wife were dirt-poor farmers living on a rented farm. Every month, Johannes had to go to the Salvation Army to get money for food. While visiting, Lyle explained to Johannes everything he had been doing in business. He talked to him about the contracts he has procured and the lifestyle and power he had accrued. Johannes was listening intently, knowing his own life was nothing like that. As the conversation ended, Lyle invited Johannes to work with the Mafia to sell his agricultural goods. He told Lyle he would think about it.

Lyle also learned during their visit that Johannes and his wife, Elsie, could not have children. After she was married at age thirty, Elsie found out that her parents, who believed in Eugenics—the practice of weeding out undesirable, heritable characteristics to be passed onto future generations—had sent her to the hospital when she was seventeen for an appendectomy and when she came out of the surgery, she had been sterilized. Elsie did not know that after her mother married her father, she had an affair with a farmhand who worked on their farm. Elsie never knew that she was the child of that farmhand until her mid-thirties. Her stepfather was disgusted by her from the moment she was born. He felt she had inherited characteristics that were not his and should never be passed on.

Elsie and Johannes had expressed a desire to Lyle that they wanted to adopt. Lyle sympathized with them, but did not know what he could do to help them. He wondered if an adoption could ever happen since they were in their forties and destitute.

On the train ride home, Lyle heard passengers talking about what the Iowa governor had done that morning. Governor Daniel Turner had declared martial law in Iowa because of civil unrest and crime. The 1929 market crash was still affecting the country. Unemployment was high, and there were long lines for food. Illness ran rampant and people were stealing to survive.

During this time of unrest, the Farmers Holiday movement picked up steam in Iowa. The farmers blocked the movement of agricultural products on the roads because, post-Depression and postwar, the margins on food and cattle shrunk. The burden of debt was more than farmers could handle. During the war, farmers invested in machinery and land to meet the demands of feeding America and other countries. The demand for goods dropped significantly postwar. Other countries could now grow crops and feed themselves. By 1933, eight percent of farms had changed hands. Many feared foreclosure. The farmers felt rebellion was their only hope. During the following year, because of the protests, they stopped foreclosures on around 140,000 farms, thus saving their livelihood. The farmers could take care of themselves. They did not wait for the government to bail them out.

The apex of the rebellion was in Sioux City, where farmers attempted to lynch a judge because he was going to foreclose on another farmer's land. The farmers blocked the roads, preventing goods from going through. They stormed the courthouse and successfully kept the judge from foreclosing.

This rebellion was of great concern to the Mafia running bootleg liquor in Iowa. With many of the roads blocked by farmers, it was difficult to move the liquor from one point to another. This inconvenience did not make Al Capone or the bosses in Chicago happy, as they were going to have to find a different way to move their products. The Mafia repackaged its bootleg liquor to look like packaged flour and wheat, and floated the packages on big barges down the Missouri River from Sioux City to Kansas City. Fortunately for them, Thomas J. Pendergast a.k.a. "Boss Tom," ruled Kansas City business. He helped them move the liquor for a price. The additional costs to the Mafia were double what it normally cost for distribution. The farmers angered the mob bosses and someday, the Mafia would collect.

After the riots in Sioux City ended in 1935, Lyle went to Lake Okoboji for vacation and met up with crime families from Illinois and Iowa for a conference to discuss business. The Crescent Hotel was the Mafia's favorite place to stay. It was a picture-perfect place to vacation, gamble, eat well, and do business. The views of the lake and the privacy were a perfect combination for the meeting. The Mafia fronted their meetings as the Okoboji Bible Conferences so as not to draw attention to themselves.

Lake Okoboji had a dark history, which also attracted the Mafia. Many of the locals claimed to feel the spirits from the 1857 Spirit Lake massacre, when nearly forty settlers were massacred by the Sioux Indians in a revenge killing. Upon learning about the history and massacre, Lyle was superstitious and wanted to run from there, but could not for fear the bosses would have him at the bottom of the lake swimming with the fishes.

During the meetings, the Mafia partners asked Lyle to move to Des Moines to further their business there. They had tired of business in Oak Leaf and knew they could get a better deal for flour elsewhere. He had already repaid his father's debt, but the Mafia had never told him, and he thought he still owed them money. Lyle turned down the offer because Alexandra was in grammar school, and he did not want to take her to a new city. Lyle asked for the move at a future date. The Mafia bosses were displeased with his request and broke into his hotel room the night before he was supposed to leave to go home. They beat him severely and told him if he did not obey their request, his daughter would be next.

After returning home from the meeting, Lyle spiraled out of control. His suppressed memories of his sister's hanging took over his mind. He went into a three-year-business decline filled with depression and anger because he would not move when the Mafia wanted him to, and they were making his life miserable. His marriage was also failing, and Genevieve was never home. The bosses repeatedly visited him to remind him of their "request," and he stalled as long as possible.

He began losing money when the state of Iowa contract he had for flour was awarded to an outside entity. As he unraveled, he began drinking and started an affair with the mayor's daughter, who most men would not want to be seen with around town. Genevieve had had it with him, with the Mafia, with Alexandra, and Oak Leaf. She filed for divorce from Lyle and moved back to France to immerse herself in the French society and culture she had so missed. As far as she was concerned, her life and family in Oak Leaf never existed.

After the divorce, Lyle sent Alexandra to Monticello, a finishing school for women, located out East, and she never returned to Oak Leaf. He knew that was the best thing for her.

Lyle begrudgingly moved to Des Moines to sell tires for the Mafia. After he arrived in Des Moines, his house and flour mill in Oak Leaf mysteriously caught fire and were destroyed. The Mafia had erased him and his family from all newspapers and society history in the county. There were no records of his marriage, family, or life in Oak Leaf.

For the next thirty years, Lyle did what he was told by the Mafia families. He lived alone and died at eighty-one, a broken and tired man.

THIRTEEN
JUST LOVE

The next morning, Elizabeth quietly snuck down the fire escape so no one would see that she spent the most fabulous, romantic night of her life with Lars. She blew him a kiss as she danced down the street and caught the trolley toward home. He was standing on the fire escape, shirtless, with his hands in his pockets, already dreaming of the next time he would see her.

When Elizabeth arrived at the Mac residence, all hell was about to break loose. Genevieve was waiting for her in the foyer, furiously pacing back and forth, wanting to know where she had been. Pointing her finger at Elizabeth, Genevieve screamed, "Alexandra was up all night coughing, and I had to take care of her. She is your job. Not mine!"

Elizabeth looked around and saw Alexandra hiding, then watched her run up the stairs crying, "My mommy hates me. My mommy hates me."

Elizabeth turned to Genevieve. "You know, you really are a class A bitch, and it is none of your business where I was last night," she said, then turned and ran upstairs to comfort Alexandra. Elizabeth and Genevieve never spoke again.

Each day, Elizabeth received a letter in the mailbox from Lars. He couldn't wait to see her again. His letters were filled with reminiscences of the wonderful, passionate night they spent together and how he couldn't wait to do it all over again!

She responded with the same passionate feelings. She was getting anxious and said that she needed to see him soon.

Lars took the train from Sioux City to Oak Leaf after Christmas. The train station was decorated with holly, bows, Christmas wreaths, and a beautiful tree. There was snow outside. Elizabeth was waiting patiently on the platform for him and was stunning in her red velvet coat and black fur hat. She always knew how to put together an outfit. Lars got off the train and ran toward her. He couldn't believe how beautiful she was. They embraced, kissed and were happy to be together again.

They walked to a place at the back of the station near the fireplace and sat down. Elizabeth blurted out that she was pregnant.

At first, Lars's heart pounded, and he thought, *What am I going to do?* And then he felt an overwhelming sense of peace and joy. He loved Elizabeth and was happy that she was going to have his baby. They left the station and checked into a local hotel. They talked all night about what their future would hold. The next morning, Lars went out, bought a wonderful breakfast and came back to the hotel to eat with Elizabeth. Even though Lars was worried because they were of different religions and had a baby on the way, he told Elizabeth everything would be OK. He pulled Elizabeth into a loving embrace and said, "I will be back in a couple of weeks."

Elizabeth took him to the station, and Lars got on the train back to Sioux City, never imagining what would come next.

Elizabeth returned to the Mac residence, as she was still a live-in nanny at age 20, and contemplated when she would tell the Macs that she was pregnant.

A couple of weeks went by and it was becoming obvious that Elizabeth was pregnant. Her clothes were getting tight and for the past three weeks, when she woke in the morning, she ran to the bathroom to throw up. She felt like hell and didn't want to eat half the time, and later in the day, she wanted to eat everything in sight. The pounds were piling on and she couldn't keep the secret anymore.

Elizabeth asked Lyle to join her in the living room and asked him to sit down and not judge her. She explained she had met the love of her life and wanted to be with him forever. She said, "I am pregnant."

Lyle was furious. He jumped off the couch, grabbed Elizabeth, shook her and belligerently yelled, "Who is the guy? I want to know! Who is he?"

When Elizabeth could finally break away from Lyle's grasp, she pushed her hair back and straightened her clothes. As she saw how angry Lyle was, she backed away from him toward the front door and said, "It is your business associate, the salesman, Lars Gustafsson."

"You are nothing but a town whore," Lyle shouted at her. "This will create a stain on my reputation as a business owner and Rotary president. Pack your bags! You are going to a boarding house in Council Bluffs that houses unwed pregnant women to finish out your pregnancy."

Elizabeth spat back, "What's the difference? I have lived like an orphan my entire life."

Before she could say goodbye to Alexandra, Lyle had one of the factory workers come to pick her up and to take her to the train station to go to Council Bluffs. Lyle was too angry and embarrassed to do it himself. However, as she walked out the door, Lyle recalled when Johannes told him he wanted a child to adopt. Lyle thought that could help his longtime friend, Johannes.

On the way to the station, Elizabeth confided in the worker about what a monster Lyle was and to watch out for him. Elizabeth headed north on the train to her destination, and someone named Flo met her at the station and took her to an unwed mothers' home.

Elizabeth snuck out of the home and sent an emergency wire via Western Union to Lars. She told him to come see her right away and gave him the address in Council Bluffs.

Lars visited Elizabeth the next day and realized what had happened to her and what a bad guy Lyle really was. He knew he needed to get her out of the unwed home so that she and the baby were safe. He moved her to a furnished rental apartment on the other side of town. He was trying to figure out how to make this love affair work with a baby.

He phoned his oldest brother, Raymond, and told him everything. Raymond was shocked at what he learned, especially that Elizabeth was Jewish. He knew that this was a serious situation and his younger brother needed his help. Lars told him he wanted to bring Elizabeth into their family.

Raymond said, "That is not a possibility, since she is not a Swedish Lutheran." He went on, "Our family would never allow or support a marriage with someone who was not of our faith. Conversion is not an option."

After talking with Raymond, Lars told Elizabeth that a marriage between them could never happen, even though he loved her with all his heart. Tears ran down her face and she was devastated by this news. She couldn't imagine how her life was going to be. She contemplated moving to another state and running from all her problems. All she wanted to do was run.

She said to Lars, "In my entire life, anyone I have ever loved has left me." He pulled her close to his heart and cried with her. They sobbed all night together. He did not want her to run and told her that after the baby was born, he would support her and their baby even though they could never marry—he loved her that much.

Three months later, March 31, 1934, Lars and Elizabeth had a beautiful baby in Council Bluffs at Mercy Hospital and named him Stanford Lynn. They chose the name Stanford to honor Elizabeth's time at the orphanage in Stanton, and chose the middle name Lynn, as that is what Elizabeth always called Lars. It was rare to have babies in a hospital in 1934, but Lars wanted the best care for Elizabeth and their new baby.

A wife of a Rotary friend of Lyle's, a labor and delivery nurse in Council Bluffs, was at the hospital during Elizabeth's delivery. She recognized Elizabeth from her many visits to Rotary dinners in Oak Leaf. She alerted Lyle that Elizabeth was in the hospital in Council Bluffs, having a baby. An angry Lyle boarded the next train and headed north to Council Bluffs to see Elizabeth and to take matters into his own hands.

By the next morning, Lyle was waiting outside her room in the hallway on the baby ward to see her. He could have cared less about the baby or Elizabeth. All he could think about was his good friend, Johannes Mueller, who wanted a baby. Lyle was going to make that happen, and he knew right where to find a baby.

Lyle left the hospital without talking to Elizabeth, as she had been sedated from giving birth. He headed to the unwed mothers' home and sought out Flo. Flo told him that Elizabeth left the home over three months ago and now lived in an apartment across town. Lyle was furious because he had been paying Flo to handle the situation and felt he was losing control. Elizabeth was going to ruin the plan he had for getting a baby for Johannes. Flo reassured him they would get Elizabeth's baby and put it up for adoption.

While meeting with Flo, Lyle learned Johannes's wife, Elsie, was Flo's niece, and Flo had been on the lookout for the right baby for them. Johannes and Elsie had desired to have a white, Protestant child for so long. She would make sure that Johannes and Elsie were first in line to get this child, as Stan met all of their criteria.

Elizabeth and baby Stan left the hospital and go to the apartment, which was in a nice part of Council Bluffs. Elizabeth was enjoying being a new mom and took Stan for daily walks around the neighborhood and through the local park. She couldn't believe what a good baby he was. All the thoughts of running away had vanished. She finally had someone in her life who would love her unconditionally and not leave her.

Lars came every weekend to see them. Elizabeth couldn't wait for Fridays at 3 p.m. for the train from Sioux City to pull into the station. The station was a short walk from the apartment, and she and Stan were always waiting when Lars arrived. She knew the weekly visits would end soon and Elizabeth was terrified of that day. On one of his last visits, Lars shared that his brother Raymond might tell his family about their relationship and baby son. But Lars told Elizabeth he would do everything he could for them to be together.

A month after Stan was born, while Lars was visiting, there was a knock on the door at Elizabeth's apartment. Lars answered the door, and Lyle pushed his way in.

Lyle argued with Lars about the baby. He said he was going to take Stan away and give him to the orphanage, where he belonged.

Elizabeth cried and screamed, "You can't take my baby! You can't take my baby!"

Lars yelled, "Get out of my house, you asshole!"

Lyle refused to leave. He punched Lars in the face so hard that the younger man fell to the floor and was knocked out. Lyle ripped Stan from Elizabeth's arms and ran out the door to meet up with Flo from the unwed mothers' home. Recently, Flo had been hired to be the superintendent of the local orphanage. What a scam! The money stream for Flo just doubled. She now ran the unwed mother's home and the local orphanage. The corruption went deep!

After Lars awoke from being struck by Lyle, Elizabeth was sobbing and told him that Lyle took their baby, and she did not know where Stan was taken. They were grief stricken, but they had no rights. They weren't married. Lyle was still Elizabeth's guardian, which meant that he had legal standing and could take Stan away. They realized they would never see Stan again.

Lars stayed with Elizabeth for the next week. They grieved together over the loss of their son. They did not leave the house until Lars went back to Sioux City. Elizabeth and Lars walked together to the station and waited for his train. They hugged and cried, knowing this would be it. They would never see each other again. Their memories would be the only thing they would have of each other.

It was time. Lars got on the train to go home. He was standing at the back of the train car with his hat tucked under his arm, looking at Elizabeth the same way he did when he met her. She stood on the platform, looking back at him. Her brown dress blew in the wind and she could barely hang on to her hat and black purse that draped over her arm. Tears streamed down her face. The train pulled away, and she was paralyzed. The love of her life was rolling away and there was nothing she could do.

Elizabeth did not return to the Mac residence as Lyle did not want the stigma of her in his home, nor did she want to be near him. She moved to Omaha to get a fresh start and knew she would never love again.

FOURTEEN
ADOPTION OF STAN

Lyle Mac was about to share good news with his war buddy. Their conversations back then centered on their dreams for the future, goals for their families, their faith, and how many children they dreamed of having. Johannes wanted a brilliant boy that he would raise as part of a white superior racial group. Lyle would listen while they spent hours in the foxhole, waiting for what was to come next. Would they die, or would they make it out alive? Lyle didn't care one whit about having children. To him, they were nothing but a nuisance and a complication of having sex.

After Lyle ripped Stan from his mother and father, he took the child to the local orphanage and dropped him off with Flo. Lyle was familiar with this orphanage as he had met with the superintendent before, when she was head of the unwed mothers' home where Elizabeth lived. The adoption paperwork he filled out with the orphanage was doctored to make it appear that the parents turned Stan over to the orphanage, in writing, of their own free will, which was one of many lies that would be propagated by the superintendent during the adoption process.

Upon leaving the orphanage, Lyle wired a message to Johannes to tell him there was a baby boy just dropped off at the orphanage where Flo was the superintendent, and that he knew the parents. He told Johannes the baby came from highly intelligent, good stock, and that he would be proud of this child—the kind of child Johannes has spoken of in the foxhole and that met all his criteria.

Johannes Mueller wrote to Elsie's Aunt Flo at the orphanage, hoping to get an interview to adopt the child. The Muellers had been destitute most of their lives and were past the ideal age to adopt. Aunt Flo granted the interview anyway.

Elsie was excited but nervous to see her Aunt Flo again. She had not seen her since her father dropped her off at the doctor's office when she was seventeen and thought she was going to have her appendix removed. Aunt Flo, who was a part-time nurse at the doctor's office, stayed with her during the procedure as support and medical help. Elsie didn't know that Aunt Flo had read her chart and realized the procedure was not an appendectomy, but a sterilization. Aunt Flo never said a word. Elsie found out about the medical betrayal of her aunt after she was married and discovered she could not have children. It was yet another secret that would destroy another life.

Elsie was thrilled that there was a possibility of getting a child. She didn't care if it was a boy or a girl. She just longed for a baby. Johannes was excited that he might raise an Aryan boy of his own. Surprisingly, Aunt Flo granted the interview. Elsie was wary because of her history with Flo and didn't trust her aunt.

The process to adopt was lengthy and costly. Most adoptions took ten months or longer to complete. Elsie and Johannes hoped they could adopt quickly.

The adoption board of the orphanage reviewed the application for the adoption of Stan by Johannes and Elsie, and they had many concerns. Johannes and Elsie had moved multiple times in the past decade and had racked up a lot of debt. They didn't own a home and, from time to time, had lived at the Salvation Army. The board was concerned that the couple was beyond the typical age for adoption and that they did not have the means to take care of a baby. It seemed this was not the time for them to get a child, and maybe that time would never come.

A letter went out from the orphanage to the Muellers stating the concerns of the board and asking for more information. Johannes called Lyle in distress and sought his help.

The next day, Lyle drove to the orphanage and asked for the superintendent, Florence.

He had a private conversation with her, and she expressed the same concerns as the board. Lyle opened up his briefcase and said, "How much concern do you have?" He reached in the case and pulled out $25,000 of Mafia money and handed it to Florence, along with a sealed envelope full of cash for Johannes. The Muellers would now be in debt to Lyle for life.

The next day, Aunt Flo prepared two sets of adoption records, one to keep at the orphanage and one to send to the Muellers. After Flo received the $25,000 and the $10,000 for the Muellers from Lyle, she called the post office and asked them to come pick up a package that needed to be mailed and signed for by the party receiving it. When the postman left her office at the orphanage with the package for the Muellers, Aunt Flo sealed the other adoption records in an envelope and taped it shut. Flo left her office, walked down the hallway, and opened the door to the basement. At the bottom of the stairs, she turned to the right and walked down a row of numbered, metal file drawers that stretched from floor to ceiling. She stopped at drawer 345, opened it, and put all the adoption documents for Stan inside. She shut the secrets of Stan's adoption in that drawer and locked it away with her key.

Elsie stood by the mailbox every day, twisting her handkerchief in her hands in anticipation of a letter with an adoption approval. Getting to adopt would be the single most wonderful thing that ever happened to her. Her father nearly killed her when she was a teenager by beating her in the head and had her sterilized when she was seventeen. She always thought that if she ever had a child, she would protect and love that person more than herself. Now that time might be coming. The anticipation was almost more than she could handle.

The following day, Elsie was sitting on the porch in the rocking chair, watching the mailbox. She felt depressed and anxious that she would never get a letter from the orphanage. A warm breeze rolled over her as she saw the postman arrive down the lane. He walked toward the porch with a bright package, and said, "Elsie, I need you to sign for this package." As she stood, her legs quivered, and her hands shook as she ripped open the envelope and finally saw the words: Congratulations, you are new parents!

Johannes was tending to the pigs and animals on the farm. Elsie ran off the porch past the hydrangeas, screaming, "Johannes, Johannes come quick, come quick!" She met him outside the pig pen and was jumping up and down. "We got a son," she exclaimed, "and there is an envelope with $10,000 in it!"

Johannes grabbed her in a moment of excitement and said, "We have to go pick him up as soon as possible." The next day, Johannes and Elsie get on the train to Council Bluffs to pick up their new baby boy.

From the Council Bluffs station, they walked the few blocks to the orphanage in typical early April weather of freezing rain and snow. Johannes rang the orphanage's doorbell, and Aunt Flo met them at the front door with Stan.

She said to them, "It is a mistake for you two to adopt. The board vehemently disagreed with this adoption and thinks it is a horrible disgrace and a mistake. I don't know how you did it, but you called in a favor from Lyle to get this child. He came through for you and, Johannes, you will forever be beholden to him and his money. Elsie, I am sorry for what has happened to you in your life, and I know that none of this is your fault. Your father was a horrible man. I went along with him with your surgery, and I should not have. My guilt is the real reason you have Stan. Once you walk away from this front door, you will never be allowed to come back, and you are never to speak of this situation. And I know Lyle told you who the parents are, and if you ever divulge the identity of the parents, Lyle will come after you and take Stan away."

Aunt Flo handed Johannes and Elsie a basket containing Stan's blankets and milk. She gave Johannes a box with all the adoption information, birth certificate, and letters of correspondence between them. Aunt Flo wanted to get rid of any evidence of the adoption except for the information in drawer 345 buried in the orphanage basement. As Johannes, Elsie, and Stan left, Flo turned around and shut and locked the door behind her. This would be the last time the Muellers would see or speak to Aunt Flo. It was the last time Flo would speak of the adoption. Johannes and Elsie were dead to her now.

Silently, Johannes, Elsie, and Stan boarded the train and went home to the farm.

FIFTEEN
ORPHANAGE TO THE FARM

Stanford was one of the few lucky kids who did not spend much time at the orphanage. Or was it really luck?

Elsie and Johannes had to adopt because she could not get pregnant. When she was thirty years old, a doctor realized that she had been sterilized as a teenager. That was her father's evil decision. He did not want her to procreate as he thought she was stupid and unfit to have children. He treated his only daughter like livestock. Both her father and her husband believed in eugenics, which was arranging reproduction to increase the occurrence of desirable heritable characteristics to improve humans. At its height, Hitler's Nazi regime adopted its doctrines.

Stan's adoptive father believed in the law for the Prevention of Progeny with Hereditary Diseases. The basics of this law were that people were sterilized for having undesirable hereditary conditions. This belief of Stan's father also carried over in his work as an agricultural researcher in swine improvement at the local university, where he worked part-time while farming. The research had a goal of combining, genetically, the best traits of a swine breed into a single genetic strain. Johannes's work haunted Elsie, especially after learning her Aunt Flo was part of her sterilization.

Because Elsie was sterilized, the lack of estrogen had decayed her body significantly. She was forty-three years old and looked sixty. She tried to care for the infant to the best of her ability, but some days were challenging. Johannes was never around to help her as he was slinging feed for the hogs and working from sunup to sundown on the farm. The first two years of raising Stan were the best for Elsie, but there were days that were trying for her. Her bones were brittle, her skin was thin, and her energy levels were low. It was difficult to chase a two-year-old.

In mid-August 1937, the days were long and hot. The pigs on the farm were not roaming in the outdoor yard attached to the barn, but huddled in a thirty-foot barn in eight separate pens. Each wooden pen had a door that faced the pen across from it. The smell from the pigs was especially overwhelming on hot days.

Welcome entertainment and relief from chores came with the annual state fair, where lemonade was cold and corn dogs with mustard were hot. Not only were animals judged and paraded around at the fair, children were as well. That summer, three-year-old Stan went out on stage to perform, demonstrating his knowledge, showing his height, girth, and supremacy. At the conclusion of the fair, Stan received a blue ribbon for having a superior IQ and body type, which pleased his father.

SIXTEEN

TERRY

Life on the farm was challenging for Johannes because there was not enough manpower on the farm to get all the chores done and take care of the livestock. Every day, Johannes felt overwhelmed with the amount of work to be done. Since he was not a young man anymore, he knew he needed more help, but did not want to let Elsie know that. There was no reason to tell her because she could not help him.

The jobs on the farm required using heavy equipment. Since Johannes was a small, feeble man, he struggled to control the machinery. One day, while he was out in the cornfields on the tractor, the tractor's gear stuck and jolted the tractor to a blunt stop. Johannes was thrown over the front of the tractor and he landed face down on the ground. His mouth was filled with dirt, corn leaves, and straw. He stood up, spit out the dirt, and checked to see if anything was broken besides his pride. Fortunately, he was fine but knew he needed to make a phone call and get some help.

Johannes called his old buddy Lyle to see if he could help him find a farmhand.

Lyle asked, "Do you remember the conversation we had about the Mafia and using them to help sell your crops and livestock? It's time you should think about using the Mafia to help you. If you agree to sell your crops and livestock through their channels, I will help you find a farmhand."

Lyle knew if he could get Johannes to sell his goods through the Mafia, the Mafia guys in Des Moines would make him a lieutenant in the organization and he would get the benefit of protection from the bosses, which he did not have.

Johannes was desperate and told Lyle, "Yes, I will sell my crops and livestock through the guys in Des Moines. But Elsie must never know our arrangement." He asked Lyle, "How are you going to find me a farmhand?"

"Leave it to me," Lyle said.

A couple of days after his conversation with Johannes, Lyle drove to Council Bluffs to see Aunt Flo. He walked in the front door and saw her in her office. She saw him coming toward her office and got up to shut the door, but Lyle got to the door first. "We have some more business to attend to," he said, and shut the door behind him.

Flo stood behind her desk with her arms crossed against her white shirt. "What business do we have?"

Lyle said, "I need another kid. This time, I need an older boy who only needs to have the skills to be a farmhand. I don't care how smart he is or where he came from. Only that he is strong and can follow directions."

Flo said, "I have got just the kid in mind, but what's in it for me?"

"What's in it for you is I will keep your secret," Lyle replied.

Flo looked confused. "My secret?"

"Yes, your secret. I know you were part of the sterilization of Elsie. If I told the state board of adoptions about that, you would be ruined."

Flo flipped her skirt, stormed out of her office, and headed downstairs to the basement. She walked by the wall of drawers, opened drawer 287, and pulled out a manilla envelope. When she returned to her office, she handed Lyle the envelope: "Here's your boy. Terry. And he's all yours. Where are you taking him?"

"None of your business," Lyle said.

Flo got seven-year-old Terry out of the bunkhouse and turned him over to Lyle. Terry was crying and could not understand what was happening. He was scared and did not know where he was going. Everything for him has been frightening since his mother died when he was five and his dad dropped him off at the orphanage. Terry still remembered his nine brothers and sisters, mom, and dad. He even remembered his real name, Oats, and would never forget it.

Lyle took Terry back to his house and called Johannes, telling him to come to the Vet's Club in West Des Moines the next day. He had a package for him. Johannes said, "OK. I will meet you at noon."

The following day, Johannes drove to West Des Moines and found the Vet's Club on Grand Avenue near the Racoon River. He parked his truck, walked up to the door and rang the doorbell.

Inside, Guido, the doorman, opened the sliding window on the door. "What do you want? State your business," he said.

Johannes felt like he made a big mistake. These Mafia people were scary. "I am here to see Lyle," he said.

The door opened, and Lyle walked out with Terry. The boy was sucking a Slow-Poke and had bubblegum in his hand. Lyle handed Johannes paper and said to him, "Here's your kid. Terry."

Johannes grabbed Terry and said, "I am your dad now and you are coming with me." Tears rolled down Terry's face as he climbed into the beat-up farm truck.

Johannes and Terry travel back to the farm. Elsie still did not know that Johannes has adopted another child. Elsie and Stan came out of the kitchen when they heard the truck, and wondered who was sitting in the front seat with Johannes.

The truck stopped, and Elsie opened the truck door to let Terry out. Elsie said to Johannes, "Meet me in the kitchen." She was unhappy and confused about why there was a child she did not know standing in the lane. "What have you done?" she demanded. "How old is this kid?"

"He is seven and the details of where I got him are none of your concern. I needed a farmhand and got one," Johannes said. "You just have to make sure he is clean and fed. And if there is any other conversation about this, there will be hell to pay."

On the farm, Stan's job was to learn, and his brother's job was to farm. Stan's mother was his nurturer and teacher and had a brilliant mind. She shared her love of music and books with him. Her imagination about travel and life sparked a desire in Stan to learn and grow.

Stan finished school two years early, when he was sixteen. His superior IQ played out well for him in his education. For many years, Elsie had written to the orphanage, describing to them how brilliant Stan was and how proud she was of his accomplishments and academic superiority. No one at the orphanage ever responded or asked about Terry.

From the time Stan was a little boy, he and his mom had talked about his future, dreams, and what she desired for him. Coming from a poor farming family, Stan had few opportunities for college or a profitable future. Elsie gave up on having Stan near her when she realized she had taught him all she could and that he needed new and more challenging opportunities.

The Korean War was just underway. Terry had left the farm two years earlier and enlisted in the Air Force. Elsie encouraged Stan to volunteer because she knew that leaving the farm would give him new opportunities. By choosing to volunteer during the national draft, Stan had the chance to choose his career field, his unit, and place of assignment. He ended up at Fort Hood, Texas, and then was stationed in Germany for four years. He was assigned to the Strategic Army Corps (STRAC) to protect American interests wherever needed. Stan had never been this far from home.

The stress of unfamiliar surroundings brought out his wild temper. Stan could never understand why he had a temper. It always upset him, knowing he could lose control and see red. One night at a pub in Hamburg, Germany, Stan drank more beer than anyone in his unit and picked fights with the locals. This reflected poorly on the unit.

As his army mates tried to intervene, the locals beat Stan so badly that he had to be taken to the hospital. The injury to his forehead was so severe that he blacked out on the way to the Army hospital. His commanding officer was awakened during the night to get Stan out of the hospital. The CO was furious. Stan being beaten up and in the hospital was a poor reflection on the CO and the unit. For the next thirty days, Stan's punishment was to be on KP duty, peeling potatoes from dawn until dusk. He was too tired to fight!

After four years of serving his country, Stan returned to the farm and took advantage of the GI Bill to attend college. While getting his undergraduate degree, he played defensive tackle for the Iowa State University football team. A stellar player with a bit of a temper, he had an edge over his opponents. With his daredevil attitude, he often took daring chances on the field, and his body paid the price for it. The biggest price was the head injury he sustained during a football game against the team's archrival. Stan was tackling the quarterback, and the opposing team center kneed Stan in his right temple. The pain was so severe that he had to be carried off the field. He did not regain consciousness for two days and his football career was over. Unfortunately for Stan, the head injuries were mounting up.

Stan returned to the farm to rest and recover from the injury. He still has a few classes to complete before graduating. Elsie was concerned for her son, and Johannes was unhappy and shared his disappointment that Stan was no longer the star on the football team. No matter what Stan had done in his life—excellent student, early graduate, soldier, college student, star football player—it was never enough. For Johannes, it was all reflected glory and now that was gone!

During the next few weeks, Johannes was intolerable to Stan and Elsie. They were accustomed to this behavior from Johannes, as he had been taking out his anger on the two of them for years. But since Stan's head injury, Johannes's temper has escalated. He was tired, frustrated, and old, and he took out his frustration physically on Elsie, who could not defend herself.

One day, after working the pigs, Johannes came into the house and found supper was not ready. Elsie was lying in bed upstairs with a headache so severe that she had trouble seeing. He ran upstairs and swung open the bedroom door, dragged her off the bed, and berated her. "Why is my dinner not ready?" He pulled her toward the stairs, still screaming at her. He smacked her in the face. She lost her balance and fell down the stairs. Johannes came down the stairs, stepped over her, and walked outside.

Elsie lay there all afternoon, in pain and afraid to move. When Stan came home from class, he found his mother at the bottom of the stairs. Johannes was out doing nightly chores. Stan ran to his mother and asked her, "What happened? What are you doing at the bottom of the stairs?"

He knelt for a closer look and saw her black and blue face.

Stan knew Johannes had always taken his frustrations out on Elsie because she was weak and would not fight back. Stan picked his mother up and gently laid her down on the living room couch. She could hardly move and hoped nothing was broken.

While Johannes was away from the house tending the animals, Elsie took Stan by the hand and begged him to leave the farm and not come back.

"No, Mom. I can't leave you here by yourself. Terry is gone, and you want me to leave you here with that monster outside?"

Elsie nodded. "Yes, that is what will be the best for everyone. Honey, my time on this earth is borrowed and my faith in God is great."

With a heavy heart and flowing tears, Stan said, "OK, Mom. I will go tomorrow."

The next morning, before Johannes woke up, Stan threw his belongings, schoolbooks, and the books he and Elsie shared into his car and drove away.

SEVENTEEN
NEW BEGINNING

After leaving the farm, Stan couldn't decide what to do with his life. He was lost and confused about the direction he should go. Should he go to school, work at a gas station or factory, or just get the hell out of that place?

Eventually, Stan enrolled in the rival school down the road from his old university. He missed his mom, but he was trying to leave that life behind.

His new school was wonderful and academically challenging. The political science major he chose was fulfilling and one he easily mastered. It provided chances for debates and intellectual discourse.

The social life at school was planned and pleasant. Stan joined a fraternity where liquor flowed and girls were everywhere. Weekend football games and parties were a blast—a far cry from the dull days at the farm. Homecoming weekend was around the corner, and Stan was looking forward to the activities. Stan's fraternity was matched up with a sorority to build a homecoming float together. When Stan walked into the big red barn right off campus to work on the float, he immediately noticed a tall, beautiful brunette with legs that never stopped. He leaned up against the barn post and watched her from afar.

She didn't notice him until her best friend whispered, "There is a tall, dark and handsome guy checking you out."

The brunette gave him a look that made Stan believe he might have a chance. He picked up some of the float flowers and walked quietly toward the gorgeous woman. He stood behind her and waited for her to turn around.

She could feel his warm breath on her neck and turned to find him there. Secretly, her heart missed a beat, and she knew then that this guy was for her. Stan introduced himself, although she barely heard a word. Somehow, she muttered, "Hi, I'm Saundra."

That night, after they finished building the floats, they went to the Brown Bottle for pizza and a beer. Most of their classmates were also at the Brown Bottle, but neither of them noticed anyone else in the bar.

Saundra woke up the next day to a phone call from Stan. He picked her up in his car and took her down by the river for a picnic lunch. The scarf gently draped over her shoulders matched the pedal pusher pants she wore, and it all made a beautiful picture.

They spent hours talking and getting to know each other. Stan finally had met someone who was an intellectual match for him. He had been craving this his entire life. He recalled times during his youth when he realized he was smarter than his parents. His conversations with Saundra reached heights he never imagined possible. She was intriguing and challenging and he loved it! Before they knew it, it was time to go. She had to be back for a mandatory sorority dinner. Stan drove as fast as he could so she wouldn't be late.

The fall flew by fast, and Stan and Saundra were inseparable. Christmas came and Stan had a big surprise! He got down on one knee and professed his love for her. Stan told Saundra that he wanted to spend the rest of his life with her. He proposed marriage, and she said yes.

They drove to her hometown in Illinois to meet her parents and brother and to share their surprise with them. Her mother, Mary, was not impressed when she met Stan. She was thinking he was not what she had planned for her daughter. *He is not a local boy and I don't know what kind of society class Stan and his parents are from.* She realized at that moment that she had lost Saundra and any control she had over her. Mary spent her days at the club playing cards, having cocktails, and smoking with the other society ladies. Their husbands were all bankers, doctors, and lawyers. Her husband was a doctor.

The night Stan and Saundra arrived, they found Saundra's father, Clarence, outside on the porch cooking steaks on the Hasty Bake, with a highball nearby and a cigarette in his hand. Her father barely said hello as he was a quiet man.

Over dinner, the two could not contain their excitement. Saundra looked at her dad and blurted out, "We are engaged!"

"Holy hell!" her mother said. "You can't do this. You are only a freshman in college. I had plans for you."

"That doesn't matter, Mother," Saundra said. "I have been at a boarding school since I was fourteen. Remember, you sent me away when my brother, your precious baby boy, was two? What do you care about what I do? You never have! My life has never been important to you and never will be!"

Stan could hardly believe what was happening and found it hard to breathe. This was not how he wanted his first meeting with Saundra's parents to go.

Saundra pushed back from the table and said, "Goodbye, Mother." She and Stan walked out the front door and drove back to school.

Two months later, they eloped and were married by their best friend, Bill, a practicing military minister whom Stan met while playing football in college. Saundra's best friend, Sally, was her matron of honor. Sally and Saundra met at boarding school when they were fourteen. So much had happened since that time when they dreamed of this day. Sally always said to Saundra, "Your life is like Camelot." Now, the fairytale was coming true, and Saundra married the man of her dreams.

Eleven months later, Stan and Saundra welcomed a beautiful baby girl into the world. Life had changed for them.

A few months later, Stan's father and Saundra's mother came to their apartment to meet their granddaughter. Elsie was not able to travel and Clarence had patients to see. Saundra had little to say to her mother, but her mother had plenty to say. After meeting Stan's father, she said in private to Saundra, "No way is Stan his son. That man is short, ugly, and old, can barely string together two sentences, and looks nothing like Stan."

Both their parents left and Saundra shared with Stan what her mother said about his father. Stan did not know what she was talking about. He called his father, and said, "Saundra's mother said there is no way you are my father. Is that true?"

The silence on the phone went on for some time. Stan said, "I asked you a question. Is this true?"

"Yes," his father finally said. "You were adopted in 1934."

Stan's head began to spin. His entire life has just been turned upside down, sideways, and backward. He felt the bile rise in his throat. "How could you lie to me my entire life? Everything is a lie. My brother, my mother, you! They're all a lie! Who are my parents? Where was I born?"

His father said, "I don't know. The orphanage we got you from burned, so there are no records of anything. I am sorry. That is just the way it is."

"Is my brother adopted, too?"

"Yes, he was adopted, too, and his records burned as well."

Stan hung up the phone and panic set in. Saundra did not know what to do to help him. With his mind spinning, Stan finally sat down. He looked at Saundra and then cradled his head in his hands and cried. "What has happened to me? I am not who I thought I was."

Saundra was upset with her mother for saying that Stan's parents could not be his parents. She believed her mother should have kept her thoughts to herself. But she never did. Her mother had opened a can of worms and those worms could not be put back in.

Saundra sat next to Stan, looked into his eyes and said, "I am so sorry. I love you with all my heart. We will get through this together."

They embraced and consoled each other. "I cannot figure out what to do or think," Stan said. "This secret and betrayal by my parents may have changed my life forever."

EIGHTEEN
FRESH START

After losing her son and watching the love of her life disappear down the train tracks, all Elizabeth wanted to do was get a fresh start. She hoped the pain of her loss would someday go away.

A secretarial job opened up at a pharmacy in Omaha, and Elizabeth applied and began work right away. The job was boring, but it paid well. After working at the flour mill, this job was a piece of cake. All she wanted to do was go to work, go home, and be left alone. She lived above a grocery and candy store and her home was within walking distance of restaurants and shopping. She had everything she needed and was content with her life.

She did not expect what came next.

A young pharmacy student from Creighton entered the drugstore to apply for an internship. As he breezed by Elizabeth's desk toward the pharmacist, he smelled the most amazing perfume. His gait slowed, and he turned his head to see who was at the desk. He glanced at the most beautiful girl he had ever seen, but kept walking. He thought, *After my interview, I will introduce myself.*

After the interview, Dick walked to the desk but found no one there. *Oh crap,* he thought. *I really wanted to meet her.*

Closer to quitting time, Dick returned to the pharmacy, intending to meet that lovely girl. He strolled through the door, saw her at her desk, and walked up to her. "Hi. I'm Dick McCall," he said. The woman was even more beautiful than he remembered and smelled so good.

Elizabeth wasn't too impressed with the introduction, but thought it was nice to meet and talk to someone her age.

Dick motioned to Elizabeth that he was going to sit on the edge of her silver metal desk. Before she gave permission, he came around the edge and sat down in front of her. He cocked his head and said, "Are you new to town?"

Elizabeth thought, *I have my own secrets, and I certainly will not share those with a stranger.* She replied, "Not really. It's nice to meet you, but I have to clock out and go home." With that, she picked up her purse and was gone.

About a week later, Dick went back to the pharmacy to accept the internship, and he asked if Elizabeth would have coffee with him on Saturday. She accepted his invitation and thus began a long courtship.

Dick was a brilliant man who graduated with two doctorate degrees, one in pharmacy and one in podiatry. His education was appealing to Elizabeth because she thought he could provide the security she had never had in her life. This could be a blessing, and Elizabeth hoped their relationship would grow.

After graduating from pharmacy school, Dick took Elizabeth to Ross's Steakhouse to celebrate. Before dessert, he got down on one knee, opened a beautiful box with a two-carat sapphire and diamond ring and proposed to Elizabeth. She fell out of her chair, hugged him, and said, "Yes, I will marry you!"

A month later, he took her to Denver for a mountaintop wedding. Elizabeth had her fresh start. She didn't tell Dick about Lars or Stan. That life was dead to her.

Dick and Elizabeth begin their new life in Nebraska City, Nebraska, where Dick opened up a pharmacy downtown and Elizabeth was settling into life as a doctor's wife. Their house was a few blocks from downtown, which made it convenient for Dick to walk to and from work.

In the evenings, Elizabeth and Dick took walks, admiring all the old trees and homes in their neighborhood. Both felt fortunate for their new life and everything they had to look forward to.

Yet Elizabeth felt an emptiness inside her. She wanted to have a baby and be the mother she always hoped to be. She and Dick dreamed of having a baby or many babies. They loved each other, and the security that Dick brought to Elizabeth meant more than love to her.

Six years after Stan's birth, Reuben McCall was born. He was a healthy, nine-pound boy. Reuben's dad was a proud papa. All their dreams had come true: a great marriage, a beautiful family, and a thriving business. Who could want more?

A week after Reuben was born, mother and son were ready to leave the hospital. Elizabeth's doctor was making his final rounds for the day. He visited with Elizabeth and Reube and was feeling great about letting his patients leave the hospital. Elizabeth wore a beautiful spring dress, and she was glowing. Reube lay in her arms, wrapped in a blanket and ready to go into the world.

On the way out of Elizabeth's hospital room, Dr. Sells ran into Elizabeth's husband and asked if had a moment to visit. They stepped into the hallway. The doctor asked Dick, "Did you tell me that this is your first baby?"

Dick said, "Yes it is."

"Well," the doctor said, "I have to tell you that this isn't your wife's first child."

Dick felt like he had been hit with a baseball bat in his gut. It took a second for him to recover, then he asked Dr. Sells, "How do you know that?"

The doctor explained in medical detail how he knew that this was his wife's second baby. Dr. Sells, dressed in his long, white coat, backed away and put his hand on Dick's shoulder. "Son, I wish you the best."

Dick went into the hospital room where Elizabeth and Reube were sitting and barked, "Let's go!" As Dick whisked them out of the hospital room, the charge nurse, who had overheard the conversation Dick had with Dr. Sells, thought to herself, *Oh boy, that conversation is going to be bad.*

The car ride from the hospital to their home was quiet and long. Elizabeth could not figure out why Dick was so quiet. She thought he must be overwhelmed with a new baby and had a lot to think about.

When they arrived home, Dick said, "I will be back in a little while."

As the hours went by, Elizabeth kept looking out the window for him to return. At three a.m., Elizabeth got up out of bed to see if her husband was home yet, but he was not. Reube woke up crying and hungry. Elizabeth was all on her own.

She was still experiencing some post-delivery issues, and it was challenging caring for Reube on her own. The week went on, and Elizabeth did not know where Dick was. She was running out of money. Was he ever going to come back? She called the local sheriff and asked him to find out if something had happened to Dick. She thought of all the bad things that could have happened. What if he was in a car wreck or in some weird accident?

The sheriff called Elizabeth back the next day and told her there was no sign of foul play and that she would just have to wait until her husband came home.

Dick did not return home for a week.

Elizabeth heard a car door slam in the driveway. Dick walked in the door and started screaming at her. "You whore! You liar! Why did you lie to me and not tell me about having a baby before we met? This has ruined everything."

He hauled back, raising his hand, and punched Elizabeth in the face, knocking her to the floor. From the nursery, Reube heard the noise and was crying and screaming. Elizabeth couldn't get up because Dick was kicking her and dragging her across the floor.

"Dr. Sells told me at the hospital you had a baby before Reube. He could tell that when you gave birth. That you had given birth before. Is that true?" Elizabeth nodded, and Dick screamed again, "You whore!"

Elizabeth could hardly breathe. Her mouth was bleeding, and she suspected one of her ribs was broken. She couldn't get up off the floor.

Dick walked out and slammed the door, leaving to go see his longtime girlfriend, Lady Frances. He had been with her for the past week. He was in a rage and could barely see to drive.

After Dick walked out of the house, Elizabeth dragged herself toward the phone in the kitchen. She was in severe pain and could barely breathe. She knew she needed help and the only doctor she knew was Dr. Sells. It took Elizabeth almost an hour to crawl ten feet to the phone. By the time she got there, she could hardly dial because she was so weak. She was trying to remember the phone number but couldn't. Elizabeth dialed zero and Shirley, the operator, connected her to Dr. Sells at home. She told him what happened, and the doctor assured her he was on his way to her house.

Dr. Sells brought his wife along because he did not know what he was going to walk into. When they pulled into Elizabeth's driveway, they heard Reube crying. His cry was so loud that even Mrs. Sells worried something bad had happened.

They opened the front door and walked in to see blood on the floor and Elizabeth lying on the kitchen floor. Mrs. Sells ran to the baby and Dr. Sells ran toward Elizabeth to render help.

"What happened?" he asked.

Elizabeth said, "Because you told Dick about my previous birth, he left me right after Reube and I got home from the hospital and then tonight came back to the house and beat me up. He has abandoned me and Reube and is at Lady Frances's home. Because of you, I am in this situation."

Dr. Sells, with eyes full of tears, said, "I am so sorry." He put his arms around her and helped her stand so that he could help her with the broken rib and split lip. He bandaged her up, and Mrs.

Sells brought Reube into the kitchen to see his mother and get some milk.

Dr. Sells pulled his wife aside and said, "We need to help this woman. It's my fault what has happened to her," He told his wife why, and she said, "They will come home with us."

Reube and Elizabeth spent three months with Dr. and Mrs. Sells. They helped Elizabeth recover from her injuries, helping her get stronger as they knew going back home with Dick would be challenging. As the months passed, Dick spent most of his time with Lady Frances and was not affectionate toward Elizabeth. He provided a small allowance for food so that she could care for Reube. Elizabeth could not understand why she was being punished so badly by Dick. She thought, *Isn't he doing the same thing to me right now? The difference is I wasn't married when I slept with Lars, and Dick is married to me. Once again, the secret is destroying my life, and the life I have dreamed about is fading quickly.*

The following eleven years were hell, with more abuse, arguments, and unhappy holidays. Lady Frances, the mistress, was well known around town. She didn't care who knew that she was sleeping with Dick and flaunted it. She confronted Elizabeth every time she had a chance and threw her relationship with Dick in his wife's face. At the grocery store, church, and school, she was always where Elizabeth was and made things worse. Elizabeth resorted to being alone in her home to avoid embarrassment, public ridicule, and confrontations with Lady Frances.

The once prosperous pharmacy failed because of Dick's philandering and poor reputation. He was a pariah. Everyone in town knew what he had been up to and how badly he had treated Elizabeth. They shunned him. Dick had no choice but to close his business. He was broke. He decided his only way out was to join the Navy to continue to practice pharmacy and podiatry. Dick moved everyone except Lady Frances to Norfolk, Virginia, to start a new life.

Elizabeth told Dick she would divorce him if Lady Frances ever showed up and if she was a part of his life. Dick agreed, fully knowing a divorce would wreck his Navy career and officer status. Elizabeth's new life in Virginia would be the start that she needed to regain her independence.

NINETEEN
G.M.C.

The train ride to Virginia took four days from Nebraska, and the train was packed with people. The temperature in the cars was about eighty degrees, with no breeze, even with the windows open. Elizabeth and Reube could not wait to get off the train and looked forward to seeing their new home. There were so many places they got to see along the way, including a strange city in Ohio called Sellsville. The conductor told everyone that it was the home of a famous circus in the late 1800s. Reube was intrigued by this and thought to himself, *Someday I am going to ride these rails by myself and see all that there is to see.*

When they arrived on the naval base in Norfolk, Elizabeth could smell the Atlantic Ocean breeze and feel the sea salt on her arms. While Dick checked into his duty station, Elizabeth and Reube walked around the base to see what their new surroundings looked like.

All the buildings were painted a reddish-orange color and were industrial and sterile looking. The housing units looked like they could be blown away in a thunderstorm. As Elizabeth and Reube were walking around, the base commander's office representative approached them and asked Elizabeth if he could take her to their new quarters. She agreed and was excited to build a new nest for her family.

Upon arriving at unit 8910, Elizabeth was not so excited. The yard was ugly, and the windows were old and falling in. But this was the place they were going to have to live for a while, and she decided they needed to make the best of it.

Their new life in Norfolk was much the same as their old life, but it didn't have the pressures of owning a small business. Dick enjoyed working for the Navy. The stability and challenge of the work was a good fit for him. Dick still wrote to Lady Frances each week to tell her how much he missed her and that he should have married her first. He told her he was not in love with Elizabeth anymore and that someday soon he would bring her out to the East Coast and they would get married. He fantasized about their relationship in great detail in his letters to her, and Lady Frances could not wait for the time when she could be Dick's one and only lady.

Elizabeth suspected that Dick still had a relationship with Lady Frances. While cleaning out his pants to get them dry cleaned, she found a letter that Frances had sent back to him, thus confirming that Dick was still cheating on her. Elizabeth felt betrayed and furious that the affair had continued. She was wrapped up in an unloving marriage, and it was a catastrophe. The stigma of getting a divorce would have threatened Dick's military career and income because the Navy frowned upon officers who could not maintain a healthy family life and marriage. The prevailing thought in the military was that if you were unsuccessful in your home life, you would not be considered a good leader.

Since moving into base housing three months ago, Dick and Elizabeth had rarely talked. They shared the same bed, but it might as well have been separate beds. They were married in name only.

Elizabeth found a job doing secretarial work in the admiral's office. Admiral Jackson was a dream to work for. He complimented her work and treated her with respect and kindness. Even the admiral's wife, Winnie, had taken Elizabeth under her wing to show her the ropes of being an officer's wife. She taught Elizabeth how to dress properly for events and taught her all the hostess tricks. Most importantly, she helped Elizabeth maneuver through the male-dominated military maze.

As a ten-year-old, Reube loved surfing and all the freedom that came with living in a beach community. He was a loner. His dad was rarely home and when he was, all his parents did was fight. Last Christmas was one of the worst holidays. Dick and Elizabeth had been fighting again. Elizabeth found a gift from his slutty girlfriend under their Christmas tree, and she confronted Dick about his ongoing affair with Frances. Dick blew up at Elizabeth and said this will be the last Christmas they would have together and took the Christmas tree and threw it out in the middle of the street. Dick's unfaithfulness was, now more than ever, unbearable for Elizabeth. Reube struggled to handle everything going on with his parents. He wanted to run away and run so far that he never had to live with them again.

Dick was spending more time at his office on the base, which gave Elizabeth more freedom at home.

One afternoon, Elizabeth got in the car to go to the grocery store. The car started, but chugged like it was gasping for air. She pulled into the gas station on the corner. When she got out of her car, she could see inside the station where there was a red vinyl couch, a stand-alone ashtray, and a glass case filled with candy.

She called out for the mechanic to give her some help. He popped his head up from under the hood of a car, just missing hitting his head, and said, "How can I help you, ma'am?"

Elizabeth's heart raced. She was looking at a hunk of a guy. Strong, built, and good looking. His bright blue eyes pierced right through her body. The name on his shirt was G.M.C. Elizabeth wondered what that meant.

"Ma'am, can I help you?" he repeated.

"Yes," Elizabeth said. "Could you please look under my hood? I think there is a problem."

The mechanic came over and said, "Hi. I am G.M.C. Everyone calls me G."

He walked past her, and the smell of oil and dust overwhelmed Elizabeth. She had longed for the smell of a man for so many years. G looked under the hood and noticed a hose out of place. He fixed it and said, "I think you are good to go."

Elizabeth said, "How much do I owe you?"

"Nothing," he said. "I look forward to seeing you again."

Elizabeth drove away but couldn't get G off her mind.

Weeks went by and Elizabeth focused on her job and raising Reube. The fighting continued in the household, and it seemed there was never any peace when Dick was home. Dick was getting ready to leave on a four-month deployment to Rota, Spain, and the deployment could not come soon enough for Dick or Elizabeth. Elizabeth was thrilled that Dick would be gone and Reube would be spending time with a friend and his family at their beach house. The "Hallelujah Chorus" played in Elizabeth's head!

The day after Dick's departure, Elizabeth mentioned to her boss that Dick had left for deployment. Admiral Jackson said, "Well, that is weird. The guys are not leaving for another three weeks."

Elizabeth felt her blood burn through her veins and her brown eyes turned black with fury. She suspected Dick was in Nebraska. She retreated to the ladies' room to have some privacy and felt like she was going to throw up, but sobbed and shook with anger instead. It was difficult for her to get through the rest of the day at work, but somehow, she pulled herself together until it was time to go home.

After a long day at the office and discovering Dick's betrayal, Elizabeth got in her car and had car trouble. She drove to the gas station she had visited a few months back, thinking G had been so nice and could help her again. She pulled in and turned off the car.

G came out and said, "Good to see you again, Elizabeth. How can I help you?"

Elizabeth explained what was wrong and had to leave the car overnight. G offered to drive her home and she took him up on it.

She showed her ID to get them on the base. When they pulled into the driveway, Elizabeth asked G in for dinner, and he accepted. They talked past midnight, then G went home.

The next day, Elizabeth picked up her car from G, and he asked her out for dinner that night. She accepted. G took Elizabeth to a wonderful little lobster shack on the beach. The sound of the waves, the bright shining moon, and the sweet smell of the air created an amazing atmosphere. Elizabeth laughed throughout the dinner. She ate great food and felt beautiful again, never once thinking about Dick. After dinner, G drove her home, and they planned to get together over the weekend.

On Saturday, Elizabeth met G outside the gate of the base. They drove up and down the coast and sang with the radio as wind whipped through Elizabeth's hair. G stopped his white Thunderbird convertible, a car he finished fixing up six months ago. He walked to Elizabeth's side of the car to help her out, then grabbed her hand and led her down to the boardwalk that overlooked the ocean. They took off their shoes and walked along the beach. G asked Elizabeth how she ended up in Norfolk and why she was living on the base.

Elizabeth caught her breath. She didn't know what to do or say other than to tell the truth. They stopped and sat down on the sand. Elizabeth told G her whole story.

"I am in a miserable place that I am not sure how I am going to get out of," she said. "I have two children, one that was taken from me and one that lives with me and is a mess. My marriage is in name only and a sham. My husband has been having an affair for most or all of my marriage to him. I have been incredibly lonely and abandoned by men most of my life. I am not sure what is next for me."

G put his arm around her and held tight as her tears flowed. Elizabeth realized how good it felt to tell her story and that she was safe. He wiped her tears and said, "It's OK. I'm here now." After a few more hours of talking and watching the ocean, they decided it was time to leave. They returned to the naval base and went into Elizabeth's home.

While inside, G noticed it was getting late and said he should go.

"Please stay with me," Elizabeth said.

G walked over to her and lifted her chin. They kissed.

The next morning, they awoke and looked at each other. "What a great night I had," G said.

Elizabeth felt loved for the first time in a very long time. Passion swept over her. She didn't know what to do, except to do it again. The romantic morning continued until there was a knock at the bedroom door. "Mom, I'm home from the beach and I'm hungry. Can you make me some breakfast?"

Elizabeth panicked. Reube was not supposed to be home yet. He could not see or know of G or what had happened overnight. Elizabeth did not want G to leave, but he had to. As G was getting dressed to run out the back door, Elizabeth kissed him passionately as she knew their twelve-week affair would end because Dick was coming home. She would probably never see G again.

Dick returned from his deployment and no one was happy to see him, especially Elizabeth. The fighting began the second he walked into the house. Elizabeth confronted Dick about his deployment time. "You lied to me," she said. "You left on deployment a month early. Where did you go? I know where you went! You went to Nebraska to see that slut, Frances."

During the next five months, Dick and Elizabeth barely spoke. Then, at dinner one evening, Dick told Elizabeth that he had received a telegram from Dr. Sells in Nebraska that said Frances had a baby girl and died while giving birth. Elizabeth thought, *Ding dong, the witch is dead.*

However, she looked at Dick and said, "So what? What do I have to do with any of this?"

Dick replied, "The child is mine, and I am going to Nebraska on Thursday to pick her up and bring her here. You will raise her with Reube."

"No, I won't," Elizabeth said.

Dick raised his fist and hit Elizabeth across her chin. She ran to the bathroom and locked herself in.

The next morning, Elizabeth was brave enough to open the door and could see that Dick was gone. Reube was not. Elizabeth cried out for Reube, and he ran to the bathroom to sit with her while she cried and prayed. He had always been there for his mother.

A week later, Dick returned from Nebraska with his baby. He had named her Sarah Frances. Elizabeth was still furious, but knew it was not the baby's fault. It was Dick's fault that this situation existed. As time went on, Elizabeth warmed up to Sarah and cared for her more than just feeding and clothing her. Sarah would never know the true story of her birth mother because Elizabeth made Dick agree to that if she was going to raise the child.

Yet another secret.

Life at the McCall residence remained untenable for Elizabeth and Reube. Reube knew his father had cheated on his mom with another woman, and he couldn't stand the sight of his dad. His father made him sick. All Reube thought about was how he was going to get out of this hellhole of a home. The fighting never stopped. The military police came to their home many times after neighbors complained about the arguing and screaming.

Two years after Sarah was born, Reube, then 14, decided it was time to go.

He jumped out of his bedroom window, ran off the base, and started riding the rails. He would not see his mother again for sixteen years.

TWENTY
REUBE RIDES

Reube took a pillowcase packed with all he could easily carry. He took a change of clothes, a toothbrush, and a few snacks. He had been saving his allowance and holiday money for over a year, so he felt sure he could get food along the way. Reube blew his mother a kiss while she was sleeping, before he jumped out the window. He knew he would not see her for a long time. She had always loved him and protected him from his dad. He was sure she had done her best.

The walk to the train was lonely. Reube thought only about leaving everything behind. There had to be more to life than that town and military base. As he came around the corner of the station, he saw a stopped train. He looked left and right and could not see the engine or the caboose because the train was so long. There were gas tankers, passenger cars, and container cars. There was an open car door toward the back. He climbed into the graffiti-covered rail car and sat in the corner.

Where would this train take him? He didn't know and didn't really care. All he knew was it was going to take him away from there. He felt the train move. Ever so slowly, the car jerked forward and soon the hum of the rails below him lulled him to sleep. He woke up when the train rolled to a stop. The train had arrived at the first city along its route. Reube peered out the door and saw people moving about.

The culture of the rails was a lonely one. That suited Reube, as he was a loner and trusted no one. His days were spent moving from city to city, dodging railroad security known as Bulls, looking for food and trying to stay warm. In a hobo's life, there were no showers, and plenty of smelly degenerates who preyed on young boys. Boredom was constant. And, last but not least, he worried he could lose a limb while riding if he fell out of the car.

Along the way, Reube met other roaming souls who were involved with motorcycle gangs. He admired them as they had each other's back and appeared to be a weird sort of family.

After two years of riding the rails all over the East Coast, Reube hopped off the train in Georgia near Fort Benning. He saw a recruiting sign for the Marines, and thought maybe he should think about enlisting. The Korean War was winding down and had not been received well in the United States. He was scared about life and his future.

Reube spent that night in the local Salvation Army, tossing and turning, thinking about enlisting. The next morning, he walked into the recruiting office around the corner from the Salvation Army and joined the Marines at age sixteen. He had nearly frozen and starved to death during his time on the trains. To save his life, he lied about his age on the enlistment form. Reube was a survivor in survival mode. He had heard the Marines were a safe place, providing shelter and three squares a day, and Reube was hungry.

His new Marine life kept him stateside for four years at Camp Pendleton in California. Sergeant Reube became a cook at the mess hall, and he was instantly bored with his job.

While cooking hash, beans, and potatoes for more than a hundred guys every day, he had plenty of time to reflect on his first sixteen years of life. He recalled his unhappy home life and his beloved mother, Elizabeth, and wondered what was happening to her.

TWENTY ONE
THE ENVELOPE

When Reube was younger, before he ran away, he had gone with his mother to a hotel outside Norfolk to visit someone she knew from her past. Reube was too young to understand or know the horrendous role Lyle Mac had played in his mother's life.

Elizabeth had not heard from Lyle Mac for twelve years, but she found a letter in her mailbox from him. He wanted to see her. In the letter, he told her he had information about her family that he wanted her to have. Elizabeth had not seen Lyle since he ripped Stan away from her and Lars, and she could not imagine what he had to say or show her. But she was curious and wanted to confront Lyle, to tell him how he hurt her and ruined her life.

Before they went to the hotel, Reube and his mother dropped by Woolworth's so he could pick out a toy. She told him he could not play with it until they saw the man she had come to meet.

Elizabeth and Reube walked into the lobby of the hotel. Lyle was standing by the front desk, holding a big manila envelope. Elizabeth's stomach churned with anger and her heart raced at the sight of his face. Twelve years of rage that she had kept at bay threatened to overtake her. Seeing him again brought up the worst memories she had suppressed about losing her child.

Elizabeth continued walking toward Lyle and introduced Reube to him. She told Reube, "Lyle is a man I knew when I was younger."

The three of them walked down a hallway toward room 345 that Lyle had rented. Elizabeth gave Reube the game from Woolworth's and, as she and Lyle walked into the room, she told Reube to sit in the hallway and play. Elizabeth was overwhelmed by the hideousness of the decor. She was thinking to herself, *Damn, Lyle, couldn't you afford something nicer?* The gold-speckled, fleur-de-lis wallpaper was dirty and peeling. The green shag carpet reminded her of some skit on prime-time TV, and the yellow quilted bedspread was riddled with cigarette marks and stains. As she sat on the edge of the bed trying not to touch anything, Lyle gave her the envelope.

"What is this all about?" Elizabeth asked.

"I have so much to tell you, and I am here to ask your forgiveness for all the pain and suffering I have caused you and others," Lyle said.

She opened the envelope and saw all the articles and pictures of a boy paraded around like an animal at the Iowa State Fair in competency and IQ judging. This child was one of the smartest children in Iowa, and Elizabeth wondered why anyone would do that to a child. Suddenly, she realized the picture was of her baby boy, Stan. It was the first time she had seen him. Elizabeth could not control her emotions. "Why are you doing this to me?" she asked through her tears. "Haven't I had enough pain?"

"Yes, you have had so much pain, and I am here to try and make that better," he said. "I wanted you to know that the child you had is amazing and will do great things one day. Can you ever forgive me? I now realize that the people who adopted your son were not the people I thought they were. I thought I was doing what was best for everyone. Little did I know what would become of his situation. I learned this past month that his adoptive parents should never have been qualified to adopt. One picture I did not show you was a photo of Stan and his brother dressed like Hitler youth. That sickened me, and as I dug further, I learned about the adoptive father's affinity for the Nazi movement. My promise to you is to watch over him and his future children. I cannot undo the past and I am begging for your forgiveness and committed to making this right. I promise to let you know how Stan grows up and if he has children, I will show them to you as well."

She told Lyle, "I need some time to digest this. I can tell you this: what you have done is almost unforgivable and an envelope of articles does not make up for the twelve years of hell I have lived!"

Lyle said, "I understand, and I hope over time you can forgive me. I will keep my promise to you."

When Elizabeth came out of the hotel room, Reube saw that her eyes were puffy and she was upset, but she seemed calmer and not as agitated as she was when she went in. She was carrying two manila envelopes in her bag. She did not tell Reube what happened with Lyle in the hotel room.

Elizabeth kept the contents of the envelopes secret for the rest of her life.

Reube had always been curious about that memory, and he wondered what was so important in his mother's life that required that kind of meeting. What was her life like before he was born, and what was in those envelopes?

TWENTY TWO
STOVE TOP

After four years, Reube had served his time with the military and was a civilian wanderer with no future goals. He was out of the military with no high school diploma, and it was hard to get a job. He was still full of anger and had no place to release it.

He happened one day to meet a similar soul at the local breakfast bar—a guy named Stove Top. Reube struck up a conversation about nothing and was just happy to have a meal and companionship. Stove Top told Reube that he rode motorcycles in a gang and asked Reube if he rode.

Reube asked "What is riding like?"

"Riding is like a family," Stove Top said. "We adhere to no rules, are at odds with the establishment bourgeois, and have our own brotherhood code. We ride hard. We run hard! We're feared and envied by many."

"Whew! That sounds interesting," Reube said. "But I don't have any way to ride or a job to pay for a motorcycle."

Stove Top told Reube that was OK and it took a few years to be part of the gang. Stove Top told Reube he could earn his way into the group by working on the motorcycles and doing odd jobs for the guys.

Reube said, "OK. I need a job and friends to rely on."

Stove Top took Reube to meet the other members in the gang and to get a motorcycle. Animal, a.k.a. Reube, was born. Reube was a six-foot-five-inch, 300-pound badass animal, and so were the other gang members. They engaged in criminal activities, drug and weapons trafficking, stealing, money laundering, rape, and they policed themselves. Reube found the motorcycle gang to be a family and a place to unleash his anger.

Reube's anger was uncontrollable when a fire was lit in his veins. He could go from a kind, happy person to a raging, physical bull. His mother thought she had protected him from his father's abuse, but she did not know that when she was not around, Dick took his anger out on his son. Reube's anger stemmed from his dad's abuse of him and of his mother, and his dad's infidelity and absence in his life. The male role modeling had been set, and it was done poorly.

One night, while he was still working his way into the gang, Animal was on a ride with the guys and they pulled over at a local back-end bar for some beer. Animal walked into the dusty bar and saw a beautiful, long-legged gal tending bar. He introduced himself and asked her name.

"I am Piper," she said, "and I don't like bikers."

Animal loved a challenge and said, in a deep radio voice, "You would really like this biker."

"Yeah, right. I'm not interested."

As the night went on and the beer flowed, Animal worked his magic on Piper, and they left the bar together on his motorcycle for the night. Two months later, Animal and Piper were married at the farm where the gang lived in Colorado.

The next fall, Piper gave birth to their first child. Two years later, they had a second child. Animal's new life was awesome and hectic at the same time. The 1960s were filled with drugs, the Vietnam War, and chaos in the country, which fueled the drugs and the gang violence. That, in turn, pushed Animal's anger toward those around him.

Piper didn't sign up for all that was going on. Animal had become someone she didn't know, and she feared for the safety of her children and her own life. One Sunday morning, while Reube was on a ride with the guys, she packed up the kids and moved to Pennsylvania.

Living the life of an outlaw motorcycle gang member was dangerous. Reube knew he had been written off as a habitual loser by everyone he had ever known. The life of an enforcer was not one easily given up or left behind. Usually the only way out was prison or death. Reube had contemplated an exit, but did not know how to do it or where to turn. Drugs and prostitution owned him.

The memory of his mother getting envelopes from Lyle Mac haunted him. What could have been so secret? What could have been in those envelopes?

He wondered if there was someone else out there that he should know about who was like him. Chasing something they could not see and really didn't understand. Running from life all the time.

Reube was on the rebound from Piper, and the gang was moving south for the winter. Texas was wonderful. The gang joined their sister gang in Midland to winter for four months.

Animal was working on one of the local rigs and hauling oil when he met Daisy. She was a checker at the Piggly Wiggly. Reube usually shopped for food on Friday afternoons after he was done with work. One Friday, he stopped at the PW and was going to pick up some beer and snacks to take home. Animal was in Daisy's checkout line and noticed her attractive figure. She was wearing a low-cut top and when she bent over to pick up a sack for his groceries, he ogled her cleavage.

He noticed she was wearing a name tag and no wedding ring. "Hi, Daisy," he said. "I'm Reube and new to town and wondering if you would like to have a beer after you get off work?"

Daisy smacked her gum, twirled her hair with her fingers, and tried to think about what to say to the guy. Finally, she said, "I get off at eight and will think about it until then. Where are you going to be if I decide to meet you?" Reube replies to her. " I will be at the Shell Station bar in a booth in the back of the bar."

At the end of her shift, Daisy decided a cold beer sounded good. She got in her car and drove to The Shell Station bar. She saw Reube when she walked through the door. He was happy to see her and made room for her in the booth. They drank eight buckets of beer and ate a few towers of onion rings. The bar was ready to close and Daisy got up to drive home.

Reube said, "Why don't you come home with me, and we can keep the bar open all night?"

"I would love to," she said.

The night continued well into the morning and Reube and Daisy finally fell asleep at four a.m. Reube told Daisy during the night that he would move back north in a few days and asked if she would like to come with him.

She decided she was ready to get out of that cow town and asked Reube where they were going.

"We are going to Colorado."

Two weeks later, Daisy left everything behind and she and Reube, a.k.a. Animal, rode his motorcycle back to Colorado to the gang farm. They moved into Animal's bungalow and Daisy unpacked the one backpack she brought. They started their new life together and within weeks of getting there, Daisy found out she was pregnant. A few months later, she delivered a baby boy, Gabe, and Animal freaked out because he now had three children, two of which Daisy did not know existed.

Reube's insecurity about parenting set in. He didn't know how he was going to feed his current family of three, and gave no thought to taking care of his first two children. He continued to fuel his insecurities by doing drugs and having sex … not always with Daisy. During all the chaos of Animal's escapades, Daisy found herself pregnant again. She delivered a little girl, Sissie, a year and a half after Gabe.

Two years after Sissie was born, Animal and Daisy were living in the biker commune in Colorado. Reube couldn't shake off his Animal persona, and continued to party and cheat on his family. Daisy and Reube were married but really had no marriage. Daisy was raising the kids on her own and Reube showed up at home every few months after being on the road with the gang.

Gabe's seventh birthday was one the boy would never forget. He came home after school on his birthday to find his dad in a terrible rage at him. Gabe forgot to turn in an assignment and the teacher called to let his parents know Gabe had failed that assignment. Animal took the call from the teacher. He had been drinking since ten a.m. and when Gabe came home, Animal exploded and beat him with his belt until he bled. Daisy had been at work all day and when she came home and discovered what happened to Gabe, she kicked Animal out of the house and told him if he ever came back, that she would have him arrested.

Animal walked out of the house, got on his motorcycle, and never looked back.

TWENTY THREE
REUBE'S SALVATION

Running, driving, running, driving.

Reube got in his beat-up Chevy convertible and headed back into the black hole of life to meet up with the biker gang out west. Reube had moved from Colorado to Virginia a few months back and he was not happy with living on the east coast as it brought back many memories from his childhood. He was blind to what was about to happen to him.

He set out to drive from Virginia to the West Coast. A few hours into the drive, he heard a voice from the back seat of his car that said, "I have called you to preach my word, my son." Animal, having used many drugs the night before, thought the drugs were talking. He kept driving, and the voice spoke again, "I have called you to preach my word, my son."

Reube stopped and got out of the car and grabbed his bat out of the front seat to kill whoever was hiding in the backseat. He opened the door to the backseat, but no one was there. He heard the voice again and thought he was hallucinating. Reube got back in the car, turned around, and headed back toward Virginia.

Not long after he heard the voice, he met a man who told him, "Jesus loves you just like you are." Over and over, Reube heard that voice in his head. It was hard for him to understand, because his own father had never told him he loved him or accepted him as he was.

Reube knew at that moment he had a choice to make.

After arriving back to Virginia, Reube tried to figure out what the voice of God was talking about. He watched a local TV evangelist on Sundays and read the Bible every day. After hearing many sermons that irritated him, Reube decided to give the evangelist a piece of his mind about the way he preached. He headed to the local revival. Reube arrived at the church revival and went upstairs to listen to the evangelist from the balcony seats.

As he sat waiting to speak with the evangelist, Reube had an anxiety attack. He thought he was having a heart attack. He was sweating profusely and was stuck in an undersized chair when the evangelist pointed at him and asked him to come and be saved. "You, up there, my son. Come, give your heart to God. The journey is long, but the reward of heaven is even greater."

Before he knew it, Reube had walked down from the balcony, putting one foot in front of the other, and got in line to be saved. While standing close to the stage with his eyes closed, he felt someone grab his hand. He thought, *God has reached out to me to save me.*

He opened his eyes and looked down at a face lined with thirty years of worry. It was his mother, Elizabeth, who said, "Welcome home, Reube! I have been praying for you!"

Reube had not seen his mother in sixteen years. That night, Reube was saved and reunited with his mother.

Seeing his mother again took the rage out of Animal's veins and heart. He sat with his mom in the church after everyone left, and told her where he had been for the last sixteen years. He told her about the drugs, prostitution, motorcycle gang, and the things he had done. And he told her she had four grandchildren. Reube knew he had a long way to go to heal and be forgiven.

Elizabeth told him she loved him, "But you have disappointed me, son, and you have amends to make to many people, starting with me. The fear and loneliness you left me with is going to take a long time to get over."

"I know, Mom, and I am so sorry. I have hurt so many people that I love, and I don't know where to begin."

She said, "You can begin with God. I should have done a better job of sharing my Jewish heritage with you. It was difficult to share because I did not know much about the religion. My mother, whom you never met, was Jewish. She died of the Spanish flu. Her ability to teach me about her religion died with her. And now it is your chance to begin your journey of knowledge and faith."

Reube spent the next few years learning the word of God at the Tree of Life in La Mesa, California, and received a Master's of Divinity in Messianic Jewish Studies. To deepen his learning, Elizabeth sent him to Israel for a year to learn from the rabbis and explore the history of his religion. Reube prayed daily for forgiveness from his mother, his children, and his ex-wives. He had left a wake of disaster in so many lives.

After returning from Israel, Reube worked with the evangelist Rex Hubbard, after he accepted Jesus as his Messiah. His running harder and harder, and faster and faster, was finally over. He quit looking in the rearview mirror of his life and looked forward through the windshield of life.

He immersed himself in the teachings of the Bible and Jesus's word. He quit drugs, drinking, and prostitution. Rex was impressed with Reube's commitment to serving the Lord and the way he could interpret the Bible's teachings. He asked Reube to lead revivals for him.

At a tent revival in the Midwest, a woman in the front row fell head over heels in love with Reube—and she had never even met him. She stayed after the revival to introduce herself. Around one a.m. Reube finished the altar call, and Diana was waiting for him outside the tent. She introduced herself and said, "I am here to help you serve the Lord." Then Diana said to Reube, "Will you pray with me?"

Reube, for the first time in his life, was fascinated by a woman for her faith and spirit, not the size of her chest. Diana and Reube became inseparable and, two years after they met, they were married in a small church where Reube had started a ministry. Diana's three children from her first marriage stood up with her when she married Reube. After the service, they all went to Red Lobster to celebrate!

It wasn't long until people were flocking to Reube's small church, clamoring for his messages. Reube and Diana went on the road as traveling evangelists. As he moved through the country and the world, Reube laid the groundwork for God's revelation, for he knew one was coming. Reube prophesied that this would occur soon.

Reube appeared on stage as an enormous man, just as he had appeared to the gang members. His hands were large and could be seen from the back of the church. He wore glasses that were too big for his face, but that was his charm. His beard and curly hair, sometimes in a ponytail, kept the memory of Animal in his mind so he would not return to that life again.

His parishioners saw Reube as a performer and someone who got right to the point. His sermons were intense and long, and his congregation always felt the hand of God when Reube preached.

Diana and Reube chose Pensacola, Florida, as the location for a revival for pilgrims to come from around the world.

It was Reube's chance to correct the order of his life. He wanted to put his past behaviors in the past and make the path going forward right, because when the pattern is right, the glory follows.

The Brownsville Revival in Pensacola was born, and Reube ministered at the revival for two powerful years. Millions of people attended his revivals and heard the word from Reube. Some pilgrims said they saw angels flying through the tent as Reube spoke.

The revival was almost circus-like, similar to his great-grandmother's life and her families' circuses. The choir was talented and wore blue robes adorned in white. A live band, with a guitar, drums, and organ, kept the crowd on their feet singing rousing worship music.

Diana and Reube ministered for more than two years in Pensacola, and during that time, hundreds of thousands of people were saved. Reube became well known around the world for his intensity, romance, and intimacy with the Lord. Reube had a love affair with Jesus.

He saw things differently than others since becoming a Messianic Jew. He talked daily about the Law of Ten Commandments being more than a tablet made of stone. Reube would point to them as the four commandments of how to love God and the six commandments of how to love man. He felt this was the very nature of God. He loved all people, and his greatest miracle was seeing a sinner come to know Christ and to get right with God, like he did. The revival was a byproduct of his intimacy with the Lord. And now, Animal was completely erased as far as Reube was concerned.

Reube always knew he wanted to give a fresh message to the people and let them know he was there for them. He spoke the words he had missed growing up — *God loves you and I love you.*

His mother's envelopes continued to haunt him and he asked God to explain why and what was in them. But still, there was no answer.

TWENTY FOUR
BROKEN DREAMS

The year 1958 was associated with youth, vitality, integrity, charm, and a sense of unfulfilled promise. Friends of Saundra and Stan in the Des Moines law community viewed them as the dream couple of their time. It was often said that they had a beautiful marriage, were beautiful people, and there was such a sense of promise for their future. It was a magical time, and they were perceived as a power couple in legal circles.

The secrets of so many things in the universe were troubling. The envelopes, the birth parents, the hidden identities: What did it all mean?

Stan had never known love in his life until he met Saundra. His father was distant and calculating, and his mother was sweet, but she could not stand up for herself. When Stan saw Saundra from across the room in college, a fire was lit in him he had never known. After they married, and Stan knew the love of a woman who loved him back, it was like a mountain of unhappiness left his shoulders. He never wanted to give that up.

Looking back on his life, he knew things had happened that were affecting his personality. There had been the Division 1 football career during the era of leather helmets, and all the collisions and repeated concussions. Players got hit, and they got right back up and played the game. In the 1950s, no one really knew about traumatic brain injuries. Then there was the last injury that knocked him out of football and set up his father's disappointment. If Stan had been honest with himself, he would have seen that his father never really cared about him, just the glory of having a superior son.

Stan should have figured out that something was amiss when in the Army, he was the one who always picked the fights. Heck, it drew him potato duty for a month. The hits to the front of his head mounted up with the bar fights. Stan knew he had a bit of an aggressive personality growing up but living at the farm, there was no one pushing his buttons. No one saw a doctor and certainly no one saw a mental health therapist to figure out the cause of their outbursts. That would have been seen as a sign of weakness. They just picked themselves up by their bootstraps and moved on.

Stan knew he needed to protect his head and not take any more hits. He regularly suffered monster headaches and was worried that the out-of-control actions he exhibited would one day turn on the one he loved with all his soul.

Stan lived an exceptional life until the secret surfaced. The art of deception was played out by many characters in his life, including ones he trusted and loved.

That his family kept so many secrets from him was incomprehensible. Deep down, Stan always knew Elsie was not his biological mother. He had been afraid to confront his parents about his feelings and questions when he knew it would make his father furious. The emotions caused Stan to spiral out of control and lose focus on things that were important, like his career and family. Not only was Stan losing control, his marriage was deteriorating as well. The source of all his anger was pointed at Saundra. If her mother had never said anything about who his parents were, Stan would not have felt the way he did. Knowing none of this would have been just fine with him.

One night after work, Stan told Saundra that he hated her because her mother was right. He told her he did not know who he was, what he was, and where he was supposed to be. The lies he'd been told didn't add up in his mind. He had been trained as an attorney and couldn't make sense of all this. He wondered, *How did this happen to me?*

In a heated conversation, Stan said to Saundra, "I have to figure this out for myself. Saundra, you probably won't be part of this journey with me."

And, with that, he looked back at Saundra and walked out the front door.

TWENTY FIVE
VISIT TO THE FARM

Stan reflected on his life in an effort to understand it. As a young man, he had been emotionally blind and believed in the people that he called his family. His new mother-in-law couldn't believe he had never questioned who his parents were, because from the first time she saw them, she could see they were old, short, and looked nothing like him.

Living on a farm kept them from talking with a lot of different people. He supposed if he had lived in a big city, the question might have come up sooner in his life. But it didn't. He wished it would have, and he probably would have been able to deal with the secret a lot better. But after so much time passed and as an adult, he knew how they deceived him. There were so many lies that were told on purpose to keep the secret going. That was probably the thing that hurt the most.

A month after Stan walked out the front door, Stan trekked up to the farm to confront his mother, Elsie. Her deception had hurt him the most. They shared so many memories and dreamed a lot together, and now he knew it was not real. So many promises were made, and it was all a lie. As he drove up the lane to talk with his … not parents … he saw Elsie waiting for him on the porch.

Stan got out of the car and said, "How could you have lied to me for so many years? I hate you for this and I don't understand. I am so angry and frustrated and don't know where my life will go from here."

"Son," Elsie said, "please sit down. I have a lot to tell you."

This would be one of Elsie's last days of lucidity.

As they rocked in the porch chairs and drank iced tea, Elsie told him about her life. She told him of the horrors that began when she was twelve. She had been raped repeatedly by her male cousins, father, and brothers for years. The memories of those days were unbearable. Elsie's mother knew it was happening to her and never did a thing about it.

"You see, in those days, women had no voice and no right to anything. Not even their bodies," Elsie said. She said her father was the worst abuser of all. Not only did he rape her repeatedly, he hit her in the head until her ears bled. "I used to hear the sweet sounds of the piano I played, and now I cannot. When I was seventeen, I went to the hospital to have my appendix removed, or so I was told. Actually, the doctor sterilized me at the request of my father. So, now you know why I could never have any children of my own." As he listened to her, Stan's anger began to turn into empathy for his mother.

"When I met Johannes, I was eighteen, and we got married in Winterset, Iowa. I had no idea that I had been sterilized the year before. I truly thought I had my appendix taken out. It was about six years later that I found out from another doctor that I had been sterilized, and that's why I could not get pregnant. Can you imagine the rage and deception I felt? I wanted to kill my dad and mother for everything they had done to me." As he was rocking in the chair next to his mom Stan was feeling uncomfortable and realized that he was not the only one with a story of secrets.

"During that time, it was fashionable to follow Margaret Sanger and be on the eugenics train. And, I was a victim of that fashion. My Aunt Florence, who was the superintendent of the orphanage you were at, facilitated Johannes and I being able to adopt you at our elderly age. She owed me that much for being part of the secret of my sterilization. She should have told me!

You were absolutely the greatest gift and joy I ever had in my life. Even though you were not my flesh and blood, I always believed you were. Will you ever be able to forgive me for keeping the secret from you and not telling you the truth until now?" Stan reached his hand over the rocking chair toward her and grabbed her hand and said, with tears in his eyes, "I am so sorry mom."

"Now, I will tell you that Johannes has a different story than me. You were adopted to elevate his life to make him look like a real man, and so he could pass along the white supremacy life to a child. He never cared about you or Terry. You both were just a means to an end, like a farmhand on a pig farm. I am not sure why Johannes is this way. We never talked about his upbringing and I have never met his family. I know they were from Berlin, Germany, and settled in Ohio somewhere. I am happy that you didn't know them. That was a gift. I am sorry to tell you all this, but I should have done this a long time ago. I also know that all of this will affect your family, and especially Saundra. She is a good woman. I hope that this won't destroy that. On your next journey to find out your past, Oak Leaf may be a place you want to go."

"Why Oak Leaf?" Stan asked.

"It is where it all began for you," Elsie said.

"Johannes is not the same man I married. I am not sure what happened to him along the way, but maybe he really was always like this. Now that I am ill and suffering from injuries from the fall down the stairs, I don't think I will ever figure it out. Just know, I always loved you."

Stan got up from his rocker and hugged his mom with all his might and whispered, "I will always love you too."

Three weeks later, Stan received a call from Johannes telling him that Elsie had succumbed to her injuries from her fall down the stairs, and had passed away.

TWENTY SIX
THE CHILDREN

The happiest time in Stan's life was when his first child was born. He and Sauny were broke, but madly in love. Michelle was a challenging, colicky baby but was the apple of his eye.

As Stan and Sauny began their journey into parenthood, Stan realized how hard it would be, but he was up for the challenge. After Michelle came home from the hospital, Stan joined the Army Reserve for extra income. He attended law school at Drake and was in class Monday, Wednesday, and Friday until noon. He worked every waking hour except on Sundays.

Sundays were the best day of the week for Stan because that day was devoted to his family. They came home from church and had a big fat roast with potatoes and carrots. That same routine every Sunday was so comforting to Stan because it was the only normal, stress-free day of the week. Michelle used to run up and down the pews at church, laughing and shrieking, taunting her dad. Stan loved her laugh and the bounce in her run. Michelle was so happy and always grinned at her dad when he would try to chase her down a pew, never catching her.

That feeling of joy would dissipate as time went by, but so many great things happened until that fateful day.

Law school was going well for Stan. He loved being challenged intellectually. He was extremely competitive and thrived in that academic environment. In his second year of law school, he became the editor of the law review at Drake University. Stan had dreamed about being the editor for a long time, and now that dream was a reality. Law school flew by and he reached graduation day. Finishing third in his class was quite a feat, especially for a kid who grew up on a pig farm.

A month after graduation, Stan was recruited by F. Lee Bailey's law firm in Dallas. He was flying high! He drove to Dallas for the interview and fell in love with Texas. What an opportunity sat in front of him! F. Lee wined and dined Stan and told him that in two years, he could make partner. Stan's mind was blown, and he felt all the hard work he put in over the past six or seven years was finally paying off. He was eager to get home and tell Michelle and Sauny that they were moving to Texas.

When he returned to Des Moines, Stan made the mistake of driving to the farm first to tell his father, Johannes, about the offer from the firm in Texas. Stan was so excited and so proud of himself, and he thought his dad would be too. Johannes listened to Stan and saw his excitement, but thought, *I cannot let him move to Dallas or be out of my sight. If he moves away, he might find out who his parents really are because he would have the resources to hire private detectives and researchers at the law firm in Dallas that could find out everything. I cannot let him find out the dishonest dealings that happened with the orphanage with Elsie's family and his adoption. That would make me look bad for all the deception and lies I told him.*

Johannes said, "I will give you $30,000 to help you start your practice if you stay here. I am old and sick, and I rescued you from the orphanage. You owe me."

The gut punch to Stan was overwhelming. He could hardly breathe, and he knew his dreams had been shot down. He thought, *I really don't want to start my own firm and be in a town I don't think I could thrive in. I really need to start with a salary because I have a wife and daughter to care for.*

Stan realized he would never get away from his father. He wished he would have done the same thing Terry did when he made the military his profession instead of coming home. Stan knew this was where he would stay, with a new law firm in Des Moines. *How much longer do I have to pay for the "sin" of being adopted?*

Stan began his practice downtown with the money from his father. It was a small operation at first—Stan, a secretary, and a private detective on the payroll. The cases started coming in because Stan was tightly connected to the courts and other lawyers after clerking in Des Moines during law school. He had high-profile cases that made the front page of the newspaper. One case involved a girl who was stolen by her noncustodial parent and taken to another state. Stan got her home to the custodial parent with the help of the detective. The newspaper was at his office daily for updates about the prosecution of the kidnapper. Stan grew his practice and made his mark on the law scene in Des Moines.

Although he enjoyed success and notoriety, Stan also experienced regret. The money he earned in private practice was nothing compared to what he would have made in Dallas. There was no partnership to be had. Heck, he was the partnership. His dad had ruined his life, and he wondered daily why he had listened to him and why he allowed his father to bribe him into staying. He was frustrated that he would never have the chance to litigate the way he should have or spar with colleagues. Daily, he dealt with small-town law and was bored with it. Stan despised his dad, the farm, the adoption, everything! But most of all, he felt betrayed by his father for not telling him the truth about his adoption when he was a child.

Stan held on to the secret of his adoption. Only he and Sauny knew the truth. He did not even tell his best friend, who briefly lived in their basement, that he was adopted. Stan told no one. He was embarrassed and angry about the secret and it would begin the path to his and his family's emotional destruction.

Stan had a lot of questions about his real parents and was frustrated that he had no one to ask. He imagined who they were. He wondered why they put him up for adoption. Would they have supported him? Would they have encouraged him to reach for the stars? The secret continued to eat at him. He had so much to unpack and work through, and there was no one to help him resolve his problems. Men did not seek therapy; that was a sign of weakness. They were expected to be strong and stoic. He struggled to cope and turned to excessive drinking, eating, and womanizing. His sense of self-worth was destroyed by the secret and by the past. One night, after drinking too much at the Embers, Stan got into his VW Bug and started down Ingersoll Road. The roads were icy, and it was a frigid night in Iowa. Stan was not paying attention and missed the left turn he was supposed to take. He over-corrected and ran straight into a telephone pole. He hit the pole so hard that his head went through the windshield. The people in the house across the street heard the crash and called emergency services. An ambulance arrived and Stan was taken by ambulance to Des Moines General. He had fifty stitches put in his forehead and there was still some glass left in his head.

A couple of months after the accident, Stan began searching for his parents. He began by calling his father for details about his adoption. His father told him that the orphanage had burned to the ground, and he had no information about Stan's biological parents. He said he knew nothing.

Stan didn't believe him and drove to the farm to demand he give him information about his adoption. Again, Johannes said he knew nothing. Irate, Stan left the farm in his car at high speed, spewing gravel and dust everywhere. On the way home, Stan stopped at the Lil' General package store and bought a bottle of whiskey to drown his frustration and anger. By the time he arrived home, he was drunk.

When he went into the house, Sauny smelled the liquor and asked him where he had been. Leaning against the doorway in his suit pants, white shirt, and pencil thin tie, Stan started yelling at Sauny. He took out his frustrations on her. He was screaming horrible things and profanities at her. In fear, Sauny scooped up Michelle, ran into the garage, got in the car and threw Michelle on the floor of the TR6. She grabbed a container of cupcakes, decorated like turkeys, that were sitting next to the car and tossed them to Michelle. As Stan bellowed and rushed toward her, she threw the car in reverse and raced to Johannes's farm in Ames, the place she believed would be a haven for her and Michelle. She did not know that the person she trusted at the farm had the answers to Stan's questions all along.

Michelle and Sauny stayed at the farm for two days. They had driven away with no extra clothing, toothbrushes, or extra blankets. It was always so cold at the farm because there was little heat coming out of the coal furnace. The best part of the two days was the Archway cookies Michelle got to eat. But they had to return home because Saundra had to go to work.

When they arrived home, Stan was nowhere to be found. He did not come home for the next two days. Saundra was worried and didn't have any appetite. All she did was smoke Winston cigarettes and roam around the house through the night. She called her best friend, Maeve, for support and advice. Maeve, who lived down the street, came to the house and smoked cigarettes with her. She brought her own martinis because she knew she was going to need a drink. Maeve's support was unwavering, and she was like the sister Sauny never had.

Stan came home at the end of the week and apologized to Sauny for being gone and for the outburst he had unleashed on her. His apology fell short, and it took months for Saundra to forgive him. She could not forget the harsh words he said or how scared she was for herself and Michelle. Her fury lingered about the crappy, wintry days they had endured at the farm. She was not one to forgive and forget easily.

As days went by, Stan and Saundra's married life resumed a normal cadence. He finally convinced her to take a trip together to the Lake of the Ozarks in Missouri. He hoped this would help them repair things and move forward. Stan suppressed all thoughts of finding his parents and believed what his dad had told him. The only resource he had was a private detective who struggled to gather any information about Stan's birth. With the orphanage destroyed, where would they start?

The long weekend in the Ozarks was just what they both needed: dinners, dancing, boat rides, and long mornings in bed. Stan and Saundra finally, intimately, reconnected. It had been a long time since they were close and able to love each other the way they used to. When they returned home, Saundra found out she was pregnant and the memory of the long morning in bed at the Ozarks would be with her forever. She was happy, happy, happy. Sauny believed that a new addition to their family would repair the marriage.

Nine months later, Michelle was joined by a baby sister, Cassaundra. Michelle was thrilled and excited to have a sister, and she took care of her like a baby doll. Saundra was exhausted after giving birth. Stan had become disconnected again from Saundra as his suppressed emotions about the adoption secret had returned to the surface. Sauny thought Stan was spending all his extra time at the office, building a strong law practice to take care of his family. She took over all the household chores, cared for the children, and worked a full-time job. What she would find out later would rip her apart.

She confided in Maeve how tired she was. "Maybe I should just go it alone," she said, "since I already do that."

Maeve shared with Saundra that she had seen Stan talking with a group of ladies and a guy who looked like a mechanic at the Embers the night before. She thought little about it since a lot of business in Des Moines was conducted at that restaurant. Now that Maeve was saying it out loud, she realizes they really were not conducting business. They were planning something. They had car manuals and race forms on the table.

The following April, Stan walked into the house and said, "I've taken up the sport of car racing. I have a mechanic and a loaner car for the first race, and I'm heading to Wisconsin tomorrow."

After Sauny overcame the shock of this news, she said, "The hell you are! The sport of racing does not make sense. The danger of the sport and having a family do not go hand in hand. We do not have the money!"

He spun toward her and said, "This is not your decision, and you do not have a say in what I do."

"What the hell do you mean?" she replied angrily. "I don't have a say in it? I worked seventy-hour weeks while taking care of a toddler to put you through law school. How dare you! The money is just as much mine as it is yours. This should have been a conversation we had together, not a unilateral decision."

She wondered what was wrong with Stan that made him want to race. What was he running from, looking for, and chasing?

The racing went from one race a month to every other weekend. The money had drained away because of racing. Saundra worked to pay the mortgage and make sure the girls had something to eat. Stan's lack of attention to the law practice was causing the practice to fail. The bill collectors were at his door, and his dad's hand was out for repayment of the thirty thousand dollars. Stan's obsession with the secret and his racing could lead to his destruction.

Stan continued to race and ignored the girls and Saundra. Maeve had occasional parties, and Saundra would stop in just for adult company. A few neighborhood men noticed that Saundra came alone, and they were interested in her. One of them was a successful architect who loved her legs. She was not interested. She was too tired and had two girls.

Stan was not winning races, had no sponsors, and would not win for a long time. That frustrated him because he believed he was a better racer than anyone else. He was a legend in his own mind. The problem was that when the car broke down or he ran into a hay bale at a race, there was no money to fix the car. Shorty, the mechanic, did his best most weekends to make ends meet. After every race, they barely had enough gas money to get home. Stan's monster headaches were increasing in frequency and becoming excruciating.

Everyone wondered what Stan was chasing. He was ruining his family and his law practice. The dangers of racing had not occurred to him yet. Or had they?

TWENTY SEVEN
ON THEIR OWN

Two years had gone by since Stan started racing. Stan and Sauny went with the kids to Wichita for a graduation ceremony for Saundra's brother, which was a command appearance dictated by Saundra's mother, Mary. Stan and Sauny's best friends, the Petres from New Mexico, whom they had not seen since law school, met up with them in Wichita with their kids. Wichita was halfway between Des Moines and Lubbock, Texas.

After graduation, the adults left the oldest kids, Michelle and Kate Petre, in the hotel to babysit the other children so they could go out and party. The adults headed out to the bars to celebrate the graduation, and everybody got shitfaced. Too much liquor and too little food was a recipe for disaster. When Stan and Saundra got back to the hotel suite, Stan had his heart set on seducing Saundra. They agreed when they checked into the hotel that Stan would sleep on the couch. After the fun night and all the booze they had just had, Stan convinced Saundra to let him sleep with her. She agreed, as she had had so much to drink, and heaven knew it had been a long time since she had had sex. The sad thing about that night was, it was just sex.

Upon returning from Wichita, weeks went by and nothing in her relationship with Stan got any better. Fed up with the whole situation, Saundra filed for divorce and kicked Stan out of the house. She was officially on her own. Her attorney advised her to try to work it out, but she was done. This was going to be a hard road for her because, in Des Moines, some lawyers protected each other. The wives of lawyers filing for divorce did not always get the best settlements, no matter who was representing them.

The following week, Saundra felt unwell. She has been under tremendous strain with the divorce, the girls, and work. Saundra decided she might need a sleeping pill and went to see her doctor.

While she was at Dr. Pine's office, he said, "I know you are under a lot of stress. However, I really think you are just pregnant. Let's do a test to confirm my suspicions."

Lo and behold, Dr. Pine was right. The news made Saundra go numb. She thought to herself, *What the hell am I going to do? I do not want this baby! All I want is out of my marriage and now I am trapped and feel like I cannot get out. How am I going to feed another mouth?*

Nine and half months later, Bob was born. And, from day one, Bob was a challenging baby to handle.

The following years were hard on Saundra as she attempted to navigate her new life. As Bob grew, he created mayhem in the house. By the time he was three, Bob had set the house on fire multiple times with Saundra's cigarette lighter. Bob liked the sound of the fire engines coming to the house and the look and smell of fire. His behavior could have been a response to Stan no longer being in the house and moving back and forth because of visitation rules by the court. He was fascinated with crime, police cars, and fire engines. After Bob set the fires in the house, no one in the family could figure out how to get his attention to make him stop. As the last option, Stan called in a favor with the sheriff to put Bob in a jail cell to show him what would happen if he broke the law and set fires—basically, to scare him straight. Sitting in the jail cell had no effect on Bob.

Saundra was working constantly to make ends meet. She relied heavily on Michelle to watch the two younger children, and that was tough duty for a twelve-year-old. One weekend while Saundra was cleaning the house and trying to catch up, a lady rang the doorbell. Saundra recognized her as one of the parents on Michelle's swim team.

The lady looked disgusted. She said, "I found Bob on the freeway riding his toy fire engine. Someone should be watching this four-year-old child!"

Saundra responded, "You are right! Someone should be!"

That was how things were going for Saundra. She was worried that Bob's behavior might never change. It turned out she was right. He was nothing but a manipulator of both parents and became a heavy drinker by age 11. Sadly, no one was paying attention to his drinking or his narcissistic behavior. To compound the mess with Bob in his early years, Saundra struggled to collect alimony and child support and to navigate life in general. She was in survival mode.

As the middle child, Cassuandra was stuck in the turbulence. There was chaos on all fronts all the time. As she got older, the chaos in the family became more intense and depressing. For years, Cassuandra did not speak to anyone in her family. Years went by before her family and teachers could see she was failing miserably. Reading and her comprehension were severely affected by the upheaval and by another problem: dyslexia.

She felt that there was no safety or security in her life. Her life was like a Ferris wheel with carnies running it and failing at all levels!

Survival was her best skill. Michelle did her best to be Cassaundra's protector. She was there for her and tried to be her advocate.

Bob was wreaking havoc and Michelle was trying to find her way out of the mess by swimming faster than anyone in the Midwest. Cassie discovered her love of dance and performed at a high level. Her perfection in toe dancing was a sight to see. The piano lessons she was forced to take were not for her, but she tagged along with her big sister to swimming practices and became a swimming athlete like her sister. Both became all-American and state hall of fame swimmers. They were a family duo. The self-esteem and adrenaline they both gained from performing at a high level kept the two of them from turning to the dark side of life.

Stan missed most of the swim meets, dance recitals, and other life events with the girls. He was self-centered and focused on racing and women. After his divorce from Saundra, Stan dated many women with poor reputations. A fellow alcoholic, Jean, found her way into his bed and wrapped him around her finger. In her mind, he was perfect and could do anything he wanted as long as he came home to her bed. She would follow him to his races like a groupie, wearing ridiculous outfits and floppy hats.

Shortly after Stan and Jean moved in together, Michelle had her sixteenth birthday. Her dad promised her a dinner with just the two of them to celebrate her Sweet Sixteen. Michelle prepared all day. She bought a new outfit and got her hair cut. They planned to go to a movie and her favorite restaurant, Maxi's. He was to pick her up at six p.m. That evening, six p.m. came and went, then seven p.m., and eight, and nine. The disappointment of her dad not showing up was overwhelming for Michelle.

Around eight thirty p.m., Maeve called and told Saundra she had seen Stan and Jean at the Embers. He was drunk. Maeve had remembered it was Michelle's birthday and that Michelle had been looking forward to that night.

Michelle was devastated and vowed that this was the final straw. She had put up with so much since she was little, and she didn't need to do that anymore. Michelle told Saundra that her relationship with her dad was over. The nightmare she had been experiencing since being thrown to the floor of the TR6 was done.

At half past ten, Stan and Jean, both drunk, pulled into the driveway and got out of the car. Stan pounded on the door and rang the doorbell multiple times. He was screaming for Michelle to get in the car to go to dinner.

Saundra finally opened the door and told Stan that Michelle was not coming with him, and he yelled, "If you don't go get her, I am going to knock down this door and get her myself."

"The hell you are!" Saundra said and slammed the door in his face. She turned around to find Michelle standing right behind her, crying. Michelle heard Stan yelling at the top of his lungs for her to get the hell out of the house and get in the car.

Michelle opened the door, stepped outside and calmly said to him with steel black eyes, "I am not going with you anywhere tonight or any night ever. We are done, and I no longer want anything to do with you. You have ruined my birthday and so many other things. I will no longer allow you to do that to me."

Michelle turned around, walked into the house, and locked the door. The screaming continued until Stan realized she was not coming back out.

TWENTY EIGHT
THE END

It had been a week like many others. The law practice was not well tended and extensions for court dates had to be obtained. Upcoming racing weekends took precedence over everything: the law practice, relationships, and his children's swim meets.

The nine-hour drive to Oklahoma, pulling a race car, was exhausting and trying. Twice, Stan needed to stop to replace things in the car engine because the radiator was overheating. Maybe he should not try to pull a race car with an outdated station wagon.

When Shorty, Jean and Stan arrived at the racecourse, they drove by the Pioneer Woman Statue at the entrance of the park and could see the Ponca City water tower to their left. The statue symbolized the heroic character of women who braved the dangers and endured the hardships of pioneer life. Ahead, they saw rolling hills and several lakes surrounding the park. For a track that was developed in 1960, it still had the look of a natural roadway. Some people said that, from the air, the one and a half mile natural road course looked like a gigantic in-shell peanut. The sights and sounds of the other racers and fans arriving at the park reinvigorated Stan.

This was the weekend, he thought—a big race, lots of press, and the hope of picking up his first sponsor. Wednesday was practice day, and all went well. Shorty had the car well-tuned and ready to go. The great thing was the British Triumph TR6 #87 car, which had a powerful engine and well balanced, soft rear suspension that allowed for good traction, was a new ride for Stan. Nine months ago, he had been in an accident in Wisconsin and they were forced to leave the car at the track, since there was so much damage to it. The damage was not only to the car. Stan broke his leg when the car hit multiple water barrels at a high rate of speed, trapping his left leg under the steering wheel.

Thursday brought more practice and time with other drivers. The drivers talked among themselves that they were surprised to see Stan at this race since he had suffered such a serious injury nine months before. They were a tight-knit group as they traveled around the Midwest together. The course owners held a dinner that night. There was a hearty meal of steak, baked potato, wedge salad, and Texas toast.

Because the dinner was on Thursday, a few cocktails were consumed. The race was on Saturday, and drivers could dry out on Friday. Awards were given out that night, and Stan received Most Improved Driver for the year. Shorty received Best Mechanic. They both were thrilled. They puffed out their chests as they came forward to receive their awards.

On Saturday morning, they woke up to a hot Fourth of July and dry conditions around the track and there was a smell of fuel and the sound of mechanics working on their race cars. Stan, Shorty, and Jean arrived at the racetrack early. Stan liked to get there when the sun was coming up. He wanted to be the first in the pits to make sure everything was in top shape. He didn't need to worry, because Shorty had tinkered with the car all night. In the pits, Stan was viewed as an elder statesman. His personality was friendly and somewhat boisterous. He was older than most of the drivers, which didn't bother him. He was happy to share his knowledge and journey with all the drivers. The respect was there.

As race time approached, Stan went through all the rituals of race time. He checked the fluids, the helmet, and went to the bathroom.

When it was time to get in the car and make it to the paddock, Stan had butterflies in his stomach. He knew how hard he had prepared for this race, the injury he just recovered from, and how much he was sacrificing for his sport. It was early July, and the temperature was near 100 degrees.

The cars lined up, and the revving of the engines was deafening. Stan's palms were sweating, and his body was vibrating. He raised his hand to his helmet and saluted Shorty, then waved at Jean, conspicuous in the stands in her big floppy hat. He was ready to go, ready to race.

The beginning of the race was no different from others. Historically, this track was unprofessionally checked. The race association did not have strict rules on the positions of the water barrels and hay bales around the track. Those placements were left up to the race organizers. Each lap around the track took about fifty seconds at 100 miles per hour.

The drivers were jockeying for position. There were lead changes on every lap. Stan knew to sit back and drive his race and all would be good.

As he drove clockwise around the six turns of the track, Stan wondered how Michelle, Cassie, and Bob were doing at the swim meet. He had forgotten to wish them good luck. He knew he should have, but he was so wrapped up in what he was doing and getting to the race he forgot. Stan thought to himself, *After this race, I will spend more time with them and focus more on what they are doing than what I want.*

158 | THE END

As the car rounded lap seventy-one of 200, Stan thought the car was acting a bit funny. Maybe it was the tires. It was boiling hot that day and maybe the tread was wearing away more quickly than normal. Stan pulled in for a pit stop for Shorty to look at the car. Shorty said, "All is good. The car looks great. You got this!"

Around lap ninety-five, Stan passed a building off to the left on hairpin curve number two. He noticed spectators and a cameraman perched atop the cement block bathroom structure. He thought that looked like a great place to watch the race. The course included six tight curves, and you had to be on your game to navigate them.

Over halfway through the race, Stan's mind was drifting a bit. Maybe it was the heat. Maybe dehydration. His mind was full of visions of his life. He flashed back to five months before, when it was Michelle's birthday. It was the last time he had seen her. He had really screwed up that day, and he knew he had to make it up to her. His mind wandered to all the times he had been hit in the head— in the Army in Germany when he would fight after drinking, the football hits, and many car accidents. He was always fighting, experiencing massive headaches, and feeling emotionally beat up. Maybe he had had one too many brain injuries to make sense of it all.

As he kept driving, his life became crystal clear in his mind. His adoption had always been a mystery, a secret really, and he had wanted to know who his parents were and why they didn't want him. Would he ever know who he was? Stan had tried to please everyone, but it was never enough. The horror of being taken to the State Fair to be judged for his prowess and intelligence still haunted him. He placed first, but that was not enough for his middle aged parents and ungrateful father.

When he was racing, he was being true to himself. The cost had been enormous. He knew he had always been searching, running, looking for answers. That's why his marriage imploded. He always thought the secret had ruined his life, but really, the secret had been the catalyst for his destructive behavior, poor decisions, and ultimately, those head injuries.

Lap after lap, Stan understood more. It was as if he was watching his life through the small, Brooklands-style windshield of the TR6 Number 87 car.

On the outside midway, in turn two, the car hit a bump in the road and launched through a stack of three hay bales. Dust and dirt flew everywhere. Stan yelled, "Shorty, Shorty, oh hell, Shorty. No!"

As he hit the bales, Stan realized that the cement block building the people were using as a viewing stand was right next to him, and he saw the horror on their faces. The car burst through the hay, only to hit multiple blue water barrels. As the TR6 sliced through the barrels, the car slammed into an oak tree branch, and all Stan's vision faded away.

Shorty heard the crash and the screams of the fans, and he ran toward the commotion.

The race marshal was sitting on top of a cement building near the oak tree and saw the crash when it happened. He grabbed his walkie-talkie and screamed to Joe at the command center, "Send all help and emergency vehicles to turn number two near the big cement block building by the oak tree!" "We are going to need the helicopter that is stationed outside the track. The driver is going to need attention quickly."

When Shorty got to the crash, he was breathing hard from running and could not believe what he saw. The sight of the crash stopped him cold and seeing his friend mangled was just about more than he can handle.

Within seconds the race was stopped, the emergency personnel blocked the roads, and the helicopter landed right in front of the cement building. A flight paramedic and a nurse jumped out of the helicopter and got to the car with Stan in it. They saw his head was pinned between the roll bar and the tree branch with most of the right side of his head and helmet smashed in. Blood covered his face and seeped out from beneath the helmet onto his shoulder. As the racers and spectators looked on in horror, and with help from other emergency personnel, the paramedic extracted him from the car and loaded him onto a stretcher.

Miraculously, Stan was still alive.

The helicopter lifted off and flew toward the hospital in Oklahoma City, a flight that would last forty-one long minutes. The paramedic and nurse tried their best to mitigate the injury to Stan's head but were unsuccessful. Stan's visions were gone forever. That had been his last head injury.

As his soul left the helicopter, Stan met the family members he had never known; they were waiting for him in heaven. Stan finally had the answers he had been looking for. The secret was gone, the order of his family was restored, and Stan was at peace.

EPILOGUE
SUNDAYS WITH MY SISSIE

Our journey was not over and here is what happened 43 years later.

Wouldn't it be nice?

The oldest sister Michelle recalls: When I think about that day, July 5, 1974, it was the worst day of my life, my siblings' lives, and many others. Everything we had known was destroyed that day.

My sister, brother, and I had been at a swim meet all day and were sleeping when the knock came at the hotel door next to us at midnight. I remember the smell of the swimsuits and the musty hotel room. I heard my mom sobbing next door.

When we woke up, we were told our father was dead.

The car ride home from that hotel and swim meet was long. The three of us curled around each other in the back seat of the car.

Our mother looked in the rearview mirror at us, feeling like she had been through a twelve-round title fight and wondering what was next.

The journey for my sister and I started many years ago. It wasn't just that final race day that defined us. There were so many other things. Our journey had many twists and turns over the last fifty years.

While it may seem as if the secret died with Stan, it did not. The years following the race, Stan's children and ex-wife, Saundra, questioned Johannes and his wife, Beatrice, whom he married the day Stan died, about the orphanage, the biological parents, and the components of the adoption. Johannes continued to lie and state there was nothing else to know. He took that stance to his grave in 1989.

Around 2008, Michelle wrote one more letter to Beatrice, hoping to uncover information. Michelle wanted to discover any important medical information since she was the oldest. The response was abrupt and filled with another pile of lies. Beatrice vehemently and angrily denied any knowledge of Stan's adoption.

Beatrice died in February of that year. A few months later, a fax arrived for Michelle. She returned the message from a wonderful woman who said, "I transcribed the letter from Beatrice you received regarding information about your father's birth. Beatrice could not write because of lack of oxygen. I believe I have what you are looking for. I found a white box while cleaning out her home that had been there for over fifty years. The box contains almost everything your family has been looking for."

Two days later, a nine-by-thirteen inch white box arrived via Federal Express at Michelle's home.

Inside the box was correspondence, pictures, and clues to what she and her sister had been looking for. There was an envelope buried in the middle of the box with three names on it. Elsie, Stan's adoptive mother, had secretly placed that envelope in the middle of the box, hoping that someday Stan would find it. If Johannes had known she did that, there would have been hell to pay. One name on the envelope was Mrs. Elizabeth McCall.

"Wouldn't it be nice to be together in a world that we belong?" That was the girls' favorite line from the Beach Boys song, because for most of their lives, they felt as though they did not belong. A piece of their life had been missing until that moment.

They had always known they could do anything they set their minds to. The night before they began their three-year journey of discovery—to discover the secrets of drawer 345—they attended a Beach Boys concert to celebrate the start of the journey ahead of them and to complete a bucket list item for both of them.

"So, wouldn't it be nice to know who your family is?"

The day after the Beach Boys concert, the girls located Elizabeth's sister, Anne, on Ancestry.com via an obituary, but they could not locate Elizabeth anywhere. Being adventurous detectives, the girls followed the information in Anne's obituary and called the funeral home on the West Coast.

The lady who answered the phone was very willing to help. The girls asked if that was where Anne was buried and if there was an obituary, and she asked them to hold on. She laid the phone down and the girls heard high heels clip-clopping down the hallway. A file cabinet flung open and then slammed shut. The lady in high heels returned to the phone and said, "I got it!"

The girls asked her if Anne had a sister named Elizabeth McCall in the obituary, and she said, "Why, yes, she did. It is right here."

The girls shrieked with joy from the office on the upper floor of Michelle's home. Their husbands could hear them from outside.

The men ran up the stairs and the girls announced to them, "We have found our grandmother!"

Unfortunately, they learned that Elizabeth had passed away six years before their search began. They located her obituary on the East Coast and found the rest of her family.

Armed with the information in the box and the obituary information, the girls brazenly thought they could get the adoption records unsealed on their own. They downloaded paperwork from websites to open the adoption records and submitted the request to the court. Their petition to the state court was flatly denied.

Not taking that denial as the definitive answer, they called law firms throughout the state to find help. Only one attorney would listen to their request, and she was persuaded to take their case when they pleaded they had rights as well. The lawyer who heard them was new to the state and had recently become a family attorney. Her name was Jane Saeed.

The girls and Jane collaborated to write a second brief, and Jane went back before the court.

A month later, Jane approached the original judge who denied the girls' first request and presented the petition to unseal the records of their father's adoption. The brief was written so well with the description of the girls' right to know who their family was that the judge agreed to unseal the records. They knew they would win!

While they thought they would learn everything they needed from unsealing the adoption record, they did not. The opened records only provided a clue: "The child was turned over in writing by the parents to the orphanage." No names, no direction, more roadblocks.

Not derailed by this lack of information, the girls went on a road trip to the orphanage. They still had the white box and its contents in their possession, and they had a new court order that opened up Stan's records.

They drove three hours to the orphanage and walked in unannounced on a frosty November morning. The orphanage was still standing and had never burned down.

They requested to speak to the supervisor of the orphanage. Out walked Vera.

The girls sat down with Vera in a small conference area and showed her the original correspondence of Stan's adoption dated 1933–1934. She became uneasy about their conversation. She asked, "Where did you get these original documents and why do you have them?" *Vera thought no one was to have these records as they were supposed to have been destroyed by my Aunt Flo, who was the orphanage superintendent during this time. Our family had harbored Flo's secret as we knew of all the hush money, the sterilization and everything that had happened to Stan and his adopted parents. We believed no one would ever know. Now these girls are sitting in front of me with all the documents......what do I do?*

Vera pushed back abruptly from the table and said, "Wait right here."

She returned fifteen minutes later, nervous and looked both girls in their eyes. She said, "Do not say anything. Do not show emotion. Just look at the piece of paper."

She slid the paper across the table to the oldest sister. On the paper was the name of the biological mother of their father, which matched the name of the clue in the white box.

The girls also learned why Vera was so nervous.

She shared that the superintendent of the orphanage in 1934 was F.S. Jackson. She was Elsie's aunt, Aunt Flo. That explained how the adoptive couple had jumped to the head of the line to adopt Stan in such a short period. The adoptive couple was inappropriate for an adoption since they were in their mid-40s, dead broke, and favored white supremacy.

In addition, they learned that Lyle Mac, who ripped the child from the arms of Elizabeth and Lars, had been in college and served in WWI with the adoptive father and had always known Johannes wanted a child. The aunt and Lyle conspired together to place Stan with adoptive parents who should never have had a child.

The girls thanked Vera and donated a hundred dollars to the orphanage. They went out to the parking lot where they cried, danced, and called Jane Saeed to tell her what had happened.

Jane answered the phone, and the girls excitedly told her, "We did it! We did it! We matched Elizabeth's name on the envelope with the name at the orphanage in drawer 345."

Jane couldn't speak. Tears were rolling down her face as well. Here was an example of why she became a family law lawyer.

As they drove home, the sisters stopped in the town they knew their biological grandmother had lived in, where their father was conceived, and learned of religious restraints in that community. On the envelope with the three names was an address of a home. They drove to that neighborhood and, weirdly enough, her house was the only one in the area to have been torn down.

They visited the local historical society and found a yearbook with their grandmother's picture.

Next to it were the words "Little Swede," and that she liked the three-letter word M-E-N. Wow!

The following weeks, the sisters worked to connect the dots. Through obituaries, they learned that Stan's biological father had three daughters, and his biological mother had another son, Reube and daughter, Sarah, and each parent had married someone else. Four of the half siblings were still alive. The girls sent FedEx messages to all of them and hoped they would respond. The following month, the phone rang at Cassaundra's house and the person on the other end said, "Hi! This is Reube. I received your package with all the information and I understand you want to know about Elizabeth. What do you want to know?"

Cassaundra said, choking back tears, "Hell, Reube, I don't know. I never thought you would call!"

Two months after that fateful call from Uncle Reube, Michelle and Cassaundra flew to the East Coast to meet him. He was in the hospital with only a few days to live. The girls arrived at the hospital, and Reube's wife, Diana, was waiting with open arms in the lobby. The girls fell into her arms and thanked her for believing in them.

Diana took the girls to the hospital room. The girls walked in with Diana and said, "Hi Uncle Reube! It is so nice to meet you!"

Reube's questions all these years about what was in the envelopes his mom received from Lyle at that awful hotel when he was so young......that answer was standing right in front of him..... the girls were the envelopes.

While Reube was lying in the hospital bed, too weak to say much, the girls got to know Diana, and she was the most wonderful and compassionate person they had ever met.

Suddenly, Reube was alert and said he wanted to talk about a conversation he had with God a few weeks before he got the envelope from the girls. He told the girls, "God told me I had more family. So, when I got your letter, I was just waiting for you."

Reube said that God told him the most important thing in life was family and that if the order of a family is off, then the entire family is out of order and chaos would be in your life. Reube said to the girls, "I think you have just put our family back in order by finding and coming to see us and introducing us to Stan."

Little did Reube know how right he was.

From left, authors Susan and Deborah enjoy a walk with their newfound first cousin Marc during a trip to Edenton, North Carolina, to connect as family for the first time.

ABOUT THE AUTHORS

Susan Crawford is retired from the pharmaceutical industry, married for 41 years with two children and four grandchildren.

Deborah Marshall is a director of sales for a regional media company, married for 36 years with one child.

Both are happy and living their best lives!

To the reader: We are so happy that you went on this journey with us. We hope that this book may open your mind to all possibilities in life. For us, this was an eye-opening experience and the *best* fishing trip we ever went on!

DRAWER 345: BOOK CLUB

The journey of writing and uncovering all the details of *Drawer 345* has been an amazing one. From Sundays with My Sissie and self-publishing, we have had a wonderful time.

We are just storytellers — and we are thrilled you chose our story to read!

If you are reading this book with your favorite book club, we have attached some thought-provoking questions for your group to discuss. We also hope you are serving wine!

If you have questions from your book club or would like us to join a discussion via Zoom, please let us know at secretsofdrawer345@gmail.com. We will try to join!

So again, thanks for reading *Drawer 345*. We hope you enjoyed the journey as much as we did. This was the best fishing trip ever!

All the best,
Susan and Deborah

BOOK CLUB QUESTIONS

1. As you read Drawer 345, what emotions were you feeling? Did you laugh, cry or smile?
2. Was any part of the book similar to your life?
3. Two sisters wrote this book. Why do you think they wrote it?
4. Who do you think Elizabeth's greatest love was?
5. Today, would the situation between Elizabeth and Lars be the same?
6. Who was your favorite character and why?
7. The brown envelop was a theme throughout. In the envelope did Elizabeth get to see into her son and grandchildren's lives? What do you think was in the envelope?
8. How did the authors incorporate historical fiction into this book?
9. Did see a main message in this book? How would that message have affected your life?
10. Did you feel Stan was finally at peace after his accident?
11. The last chapter in the book, Sundays with My Sissie, was a wrap up. What things were left unsaid and needed clarification?
12. Would this story encourage you to open your mind to other possibilities or people that may exist in your life?

Susan and Deborah are amateur storytellers and super sleuths who are not afraid of anything and will go anywhere to find answers to their questions. They both live and grew up in the Midwest. They spent the last eight years on a journey of discovery, and it was worth every minute.

If you are trying to find your family/ancestors, we hope this book will give you the courage to do so. You won't regret it!

www.ingramcontent.com/pod-product-compliance
Lightning Source LLC
Chambersburg PA
CBHW052129030426
42337CB00028B/5084